The
Christian Priest
Today

The Christian Priest Today

NEW REVISED EDITION

Michael Ramsey

COWLEY PUBLICATIONS
Cambridge ✦ *Boston*
Massachusetts

First published in 1972
by SPCK, London and revised in 1987
© Michael Ramsey 1972, 1985

International Standard Book Number: 1-56101-106-1
Library of Congress Cataloging-in-Publication Data may
be obtained upon request from the Library of Congress or
from Cowley Publications.

Cowley Publications
28 Temple Place
Boston, Massachusetts 02111

Printed in Great Britain

To the priests whom I ordained
in Durham, York and Canterbury
1952–1974

*I thank my God in all
my remembrance of you*

CONTENTS

PREFACE TO THE NEW EDITION

The call for a new edition of this book twelve years after its first appearance suggests that its theme still stands, and at the same time gives opportunity for reflection on things contemporary. In this edition, therefore, the main part of the book, consisting of Charges to candidates for the priesthood, remains unaltered, while the first chapter has been re-written and two new chapters have been added at the end.

In recent years there has been an increasing and welcome emphasis upon the ministry of the laity, and upon the role of the priest in encouraging this ministry. At the same time there has been a revived interest in the theology of priesthood, with a vision of the priesthood of the ministry in relation to both the priesthood of Christ and the priesthood of the whole Church. These questions are considered in the new chapters of this book.

April 1985   + Michael Ramsey

1

INTRODUCTION

This book consists in the main of addresses given to those about to be ordained priest and deacon in the Church of England. The call for a new edition some twelve years after its first publication suggests that the theme is a living one, while opportunity is given for the addition of some new pieces. One is the chapter entitled "The God Who Calls", which considers the meaning of vocation and the place of theology within the Church. The other, "Priesthood: Jesus and the People of God", bears upon the roles of clergy and laity today. The present introductory chapter contains some new bibliographical material, since the ecumenical discussion of the subject has been growing in very constructive ways.

In every Church in Christendom there has been a decline in the number of those who offer themselves for the ordained ministry. Much has been said and written about the diagnosis of this problem and about causes and remedies. The strength of contemporary secularism, uncertainties about faith, the enhanced role of the laity wherever Church life is vigorous with a kind of anticlericalism as its concomitant, the feeling after non-institutional forms of Christian service, and the doubts about the role of the clergy in society all deserve and receive discussion. Is the Church under judgement for failing to develop new modes and uses of ordained priesthood? Is the Church under judgement for a weakening of its faith in priesthood as a supernatural calling? I would argue that both these propositions, different as they are, point to the truth. But it is part of our Christian belief that where judgement is accepted God is present to restore and rebuild; and while responses to the priesthood are fewer the existence of so many young people with an eager sense of vocation to serve Christ and humanity in other ways is a token that the Lord has not forsaken his Church.

Meanwhile there are priests, and would-be priests, as devoted and as intelligent as at any time in history. This book is designed to hearten them and to help them in their understanding of their calling. Powerful currents of thought have their effects upon the course which the modern priest tries to steer. On the one side the quest of religion "in the secular" and the reaction from other-worldly pietism are questioning the traditional concept of the priest as a man of prayer. The democratic trends within as well as without the Church conflict with traditional concepts of the priest's authority. The hunger for "reinterpretation" can erode the integrity of the gospel as presented in the old scriptural categories. On the other side, however, are the conservative trends: back to the Bible, back to literalism, back to the supernatural, and let "liberal" be a dirty word. There is also the contrast between those who would preach a gospel of salvation devoid of any social content or context and those who would identify the gospel with a horizontal programme of social activism. Amidst the pressures of these influences upon his thought and feeling the priest has often too few facilities for study, a dearth of intellectual and spiritual counsel, and anxieties of home and economy to try his spirit. Nothing is more needed than sabbatical periods for rest and intellectual and spiritual refreshment, and no reform was more urgent than the greater provision both for study and for silent Retreat.

In the original introduction to this book I mentioned with gratitude some of the celebrated episcopal Charges of the past: those of Woodford of Ely, Lightfoot of Durham, Stubbs of Oxford and Henson of Durham; and I spoke of my own gratitude for Richard Baxter's book *The Reformed Pastor* as an account of "the timeless elements of joy and grief in the pastoral office". I mention now some recent literature inspired by the ecumenical discussion of our theme.

Karl Rahner's book *Servants of God* was specially valuable for its link with the thought of the Second Vatican Council. Since then the ecumenical trend has brought much progress in the theological discussion of priesthood. The ARCIC reports on *Eucharistic Doctrine* and *Ministry and Ordination* have done much to recall the treatment of these themes in the primitive Church. Not surprisingly, the report of the Theological Commission of the World Council of Churches, popularly known as the Lima Report, has approached the subjects with a certain similarity of outlook. The relation of these reports to one another is most helpfully discussed by Henry Chadwick in an article, *Lima, ARCIC and the Church of England*, in *Theology*, January 1984. The substantial work by Dr Schillebeeckx entitled *Ministry* seems to me to react so strongly against clericalist developments in the theology of ministry as rather to miss the role of the ministry *towards* the Church as distinct from its role in representing it.

In the original introduction I mentioned P. T. Forsyth's *Positive Preaching and the Modern Mind* as valuable for the priest today. Now I would mention another work by this Congregational divine of the earlier years of this century: *The Church and the Ministry* (1917). The book has a chapter entitled "The Ministry Sacramental", and this expounds the role of the ministry as a means of God's grace in conserving and continuing the Church's identity. The writer has little use for bishops, and he sees apostolic succession as the continuing existence of the Word and not as a series of ministers; but the ministry of Word and Sacrament creates the Church and continues its identity. These words seem worth quoting: "As priest, the ministry offers to God the Church's soul, as prophet it offers to it the salvation of God. In the minister's one person the human spirit speaks to God, and the Holy Spirit speaks to men. No wonder he is often rent assunder. No wonder he snaps in such tension. It broke the heart of Christ. But it let out in the act the heart of God."

In the fifty-six years since I was ordained priest, the world has known darkness indeed: the Second World War, the nuclear horror, countries torn apart by violence, other countries with the misery of poverty and hunger, the frightening moral confusion. Yet in these same years the light that lightens has not been extinguished, bringing into human lives evidence of God's purpose; and in Christianity there have been renewals of heroic sanctity in the contemplation of God and in the service of human suffering, with faith in the sovereignty of the death and resurrection of Jesus. No one will be nearer both to the darkness and to the light than the Christian priest today.

2

WHY THE PRIEST?

Are we beginning to commend ourselves?
(2 Cor. 3.1)

*As servants of God we commend ourselves
in every way.*
(2 Cor. 6.4)

Why the priest? You are preparing for ordination at a time when the tide flows strongly against the idea that the ordained ministry is necessary or credible. This need not disconcert you if you recall the immense obstacles and frustrations faced by our Lord and his apostles. But whereas they knew obstacles and frustrations from without ("if they persecuted me they will persecute you", the Lord told them), you are facing a malaise of doubt and questioning about priesthood within the Christian community itself. Why the priest? You know that in all Churches there are many, eager to serve Christ and possessing what we call a sense of vocation, who are yet perplexed about the meaning and relevance of ordination for the contemporary Church and society.

Amongst many attempts to diagnose the problem I have found much help in an essay by the Reverend A. A. K. Graham *Should the Ordained Ministry now Disappear?*[1] He names three causes of the malaise. The first is the reaction against the idea of a hierarchical authority which causes the historic claims of that authority to be progressively eroded by qualifications until it sometimes seems that little of it is left. The second is the decline of the role of the priest in society, where he is no longer respected as the man with "position", knowledge, skill, experience which others do not have. Sometimes this decline is accompanied by the phenomenon of an "aesthetic distaste for the clergy". The third cause, in Mr Graham's view the most relevant, is the current anti-institutional trend. There are Christians who crave for a Christianity without institutional forms; but, more significantly in this connection, there are also Christians who want the Church to be a more lively society, with far more spontaneous initiatives in leadership and service, and they see the existence of a professional ministry as a hindrance to the mature self-realization of the Church's members in creative responsibility.

The same essay goes on to ask where the credibility of the ordained priesthood is to be found, and it explores the *representative* significance of the priesthood as a gathering up of roles which belong to the whole Church. More explicitly the writer divides this representative significance under the heads of *displaying, enabling*, and *involving*.

The priest *displays* in his own person that total response to Christ to which all members of the Church are pledged. He is to be a "beacon" of the Church's pastoral, prophetic and priestly concern. "By ordination a Christian becomes a sign

[1] *Theology*, June 1968.

of the ministry of Jesus Christ in his Church."[1] Besides displaying the Church's response the priest also *enables* it, for by his professional training and concentration of labour he "gets things done". And besides displaying and enabling he also *involves* the whole Church in his own activity. When he visits a sick person, for instance, it is not only the visit of a kind Christian; it is the Church visiting. Similarly the priest can be the Church praying, the Church caring for the distressed, the Church preaching. In the Church and for the Church he *displays*, he *enables*, he *involves*.

I find this approach true to experience, true to a large part of the theology of ministry, and offering an empirical road towards the understanding of our problem, a road which starts where many people are, people who would demur at *a priori* claims about priesthood but would accept a practice and a doctrine which help the Church to be its own true self. But I want to go a step farther and to meet this empirical approach with the old doctrine that the ascended Christ gives the gift of ordained priesthood and calls men to it. So pressing on a little farther I ask, why the priest?

1. First, the priest is the teacher and preacher, and as such he is the man of *theology*. He is pledged to be a dedicated student of theology; and his study need not be vast in extent but it will be deep in its integrity, not in order that he may be erudite but in order that he may be simple. It is those whose studies are shallow who are confused and confusing. The Church's hold upon the faith requires those who in theology are "learned", concentrated, dedicated, and deep; and by his service of the laity in this role the priest will be helping them to be better witnesses. But this work will be a partnership;

[1] Max Thurian *Studia Liturgica* Vol. V, No. 3, p. 167.

and the contrast between *discens* and *docens* melts away as the priest learns from the laity much about the contemporary world and about the meaning of divine truth in its human context. Together they, from their several kinds of knowledge, will work out the meaning of the Word of God as it bears upon life's problems and upon the various spheres of the Church's witness. It can be a wonderful partnership, and within it ordained priesthood finds its role. Thus in new guises the old "didactic" and "kerygmatic" roles of the priest are carried on. The "kerygmatic" role still stands, for it is the presence of the divine Word and its proclamation to, and with, and by, the Church that the Church is still *ecclesia Dei*.

2. Next, the priest is still the *minister of reconciliation*; and by this office he links the common life of the Church to the gospel of divine forgiveness upon which its common life depends.

Now the priest today is only one among many skills and agencies designed to help people in their troubles. The psychiatrist, the doctor, the welfare officer, the marriage guidance counsellor, and many kinds of social worker bring relief to the problems with which people get entangled. The parson's monopoly has long ceased, and the confessional no longer stands pre-eminent as the seat of counsel and direction. Yet amidst all the various activities for the putting right of human ills there is so often a whole dimension missing, the dimension of sin and forgiveness. It not seldom happens that psychiatry, instead of liberating the patient into the realm of moral responsibility and the issues of conscious sin and forgiveness, can substitute medicine for moral responsibility. It is this dimension of sin and forgiveness which the priest keeps alive by an office which represents the forgiving Church and the forgiving Lord Jesus. He will do this by his ministry in Confession and Absolution and by his preaching

8

of the gospel of God's reconciliation. He will bear witness to the cost of forgiveness to the divine holiness, and he will remember that the familiar phrase in 2 Corinthians 5.18 which we translate "the ministry of reconciliation" means "the ministry of *the reconciliation*", τῆς καταλλαγῆς, the reconciliation once for all wrought on the hill of Calvary and subsequently to be applied through the centuries to every penitent heart. "Whose sins thou dost forgive they are forgiven."

3. Then, the priest, in the Church and for the Church, is the *man of prayer*. Do not all Christians pray? They do indeed, and from many of them we priests can learn to pray and to pray better. Yet "man of prayer" is in a special way the role of the priest, and because it is so the Church's prayer will be the stronger. As the teacher of theology the priest must pray, as theology which is alive includes not only book-work but the authentic knowledge of God which comes through prayer alone. So too as the minister of reconciliation the priest will pray, for he is one with those who are sinful in the bitter estrangement of their sin and in the hopeful grief of their penitence; and at the same time he is one with Christ in his sorrow for sinners and his joy at sin's conquest. As absolver and pastor, no less than as theologian and teacher, the priest has a prayer which focusses the Church's prayer. In him the Church's prayer is expressed in strength, and it thereby becomes the stronger.

4. So too the priest is the *man of the Eucharist*. The liturgy indeed belongs to all the people. We being many are the one bread, one body. We take, we break, we offer, we receive; and the more vivid realization of this has been one of the exciting marks of liturgical renewal in our time. Where then, and why then, the priests? As celebrant he is more than the people's representative. In taking, breaking, and consecrating he acts in Christ's name and in the name not only of the

particular congregation but of the Holy Catholic Church down the ages. By his office as celebrant he symbolizes the focusing of the Eucharist in the givenness of the historic gospel and in the continuing life of the Church as rooted in that gospel. He finds that at the altar he is drawn terribly and wonderfully near not only to the benefits of Christ's redemption but to the redemptive act itself.

Man of theology, man of reconciliation, man of prayer, man of the Eucharist; displaying, enabling, involving the life of the Church—such is the ordained priest. I have not made "pastor" one of the categories, because pastor describes the whole. In describing the priest's office in this way I have followed an empirical approach, beginning with the Church's practical experience and working back from this to an understanding of the ministry. This way of approach may help where a purely *a priori* or deductive approach is found unhelpful. Yet it is far from true that while the Church is our Lord's creation the ministry is only a device whereby the Church can be effective. Both Church and ministry are gifts of the divine Lord Jesus. He appointed twelve that they might be with him, and that he might send them forth. When he ascended on high he gave gifts to men. The apostle draws his commission and authority from Christ alone, and he uses an authority given to him when in Christ's name he ordains and commissions the presbyters. "Take thou authority for the office and work of a priest in the Church of God now committed unto thee by the imposition of these hands . . . and be thou a faithful dispenser of the word of God and of his holy sacraments."

"Are we then beginning to commend ourselves?" It is impossible for us to commend priesthood as something "in itself", and attempts to do so by propaganda court failure. Yet "as servants of God we commend ourselves in every way" if our consciousness is not of our own status but of Christ whose commission we hold and of the people we serve in his name. See the matter thus, and you find the old words are true:

> O Sacerdos, quid es tu?
> Non est a te, quia de nihilo,
> Non es ad te, quia mediator ad Deum,
> Non es tibi, quia sponsus ecclesiae,
> Non es tui, quia servus omnium,
> Non es tu, quia Dei minister,
> Quid es ergo? Nihil et omnia,
> O Sacerdos.

3

MAN OF PRAYER

He always lives to make intercession for them.
(Hebrews 7. 25)

"Will you be diligent in prayers?" I shall put that question to you in the cathedral tomorrow, and you will answer "I will endeavour myself so to do, the Lord being my helper". It is the Lord Jesus who will teach you to pray. You remember how the disciples once asked him "Lord, teach us to pray, as John also taught his disciples", and he is as ready to teach us as he was ready to teach the twelve in Galilee.

How did he teach them? He gave them the Our Father as the model prayer, and many parables about prayer. He taught them by those instructions. But is it not probable that they learned most of all not from what he said to them but from their daily proximity to him, the Son of Man whose prayer day by day was perfect? We can faintly imagine what it must have been like to be trying to pray while living constantly in near intercourse to one whose prayer was perfect, one in whom was the perfect response to the Father in praise, self-offering, intercession, and all that prayer means. The strength of his prayer would flow into theirs like the "virtue" flowing from him to the woman who touched the border of his robe. The disciples thus prayed *with* Jesus, *near* Jesus: and what a difference that made! It may help us if we recall the occasions of the prayers of Jesus recorded by the evangelists, no doubt as typical occasions. Meditate sometimes on the prayers of Jesus. Simon Peter finds Jesus a great while before day praying in a desert place. Jesus prays through the night before the appointment of the twelve. Jesus prays on the mountain where he was transfigured. He rejoices in the Holy Spirit, giving thanks for the reception of his message. He prays in the garden of Gethsemane. He prays during the hours on Calvary. And perhaps the prayer at the Supper in the seventeenth chapter of St John is a kind of summary of the inner meaning of all his prayer: he gives glory to the Father.

Jesus died, rose again, and ascended into heaven. The disciples now believed that he, exalted as he was in the Father's glory, was still near to them: near, sharing, bearing as in the former days. They could not doubt that his prayer continued. This conviction underlies the imagery, both in St Paul and in the Epistle to the Hebrews, of Jesus as the high priest whose intercession continues: "he always lives to make intercession for them". Amidst the blended images of the ascended Christ as priest, prophet, and king, which the Reformation divines called the *triplex munus*, we should not miss the simplicity of what is meant by his continuing intercession. He prayed on earth: he goes on praying still. The nights of prayer, the prayers a great while before day, the prayer of the garden, are somehow not of the past alone.

But we may go deeper, and when we do so we find the concept of the interceding high priest simpler still. When we say "he lives to make intercession" we note that the verb ἐντυγχανεῖν which we habitually translate "intercede" means literally not to make petitions or indeed to utter

13

words at all but to *meet*, to *encounter*, to *be with* someone on behalf of or in relation to others. Jesus is *with* the Father; with him in the intimate response of perfect humanity; with him in the power of Calvary and Easter; with him as one who bears us all upon his heart, our Son of Man, our friend, our priest; with him as our own. That is the continuing intercession of Jesus the high priest.

Now we can begin to see what is our own role as men of prayer, as priestly intercessors. We are called, near to Jesus and with Jesus and in Jesus, *to be with God with the people on our heart*. That is what you will be promising when I say to you "will you be diligent in prayers?". You will be promising to be daily with God with the people on your heart.

Your prayer then will be a rhythmic movement of all your powers, moving into the divine presence in contemplation and moving into the needs of the people in intercession. In contemplation you will reach into the peace and stillness of God's eternity, in intercession you will reach into the rough and tumble of the world of time and change.

The Godward movement has many aspects. It includes the use of mind and imagination which we call meditation, it includes the counting of God's mercies which we call praise and thanksgiving, and self-abasement which we call confession. But try to think of it more simply: it means putting yourself near God, with God, in a time of quietness every day. You put yourself with him just as you are, in the feebleness of your concentration, in your lack of warmth and desire, not trying to manufacture pious thoughts or phrases. You put yourself with God, empty perhaps, but hungry and thirsty for him; and if in sincerity you cannot say that you want God you can perhaps tell him that you want to want him; and if you cannot say even that perhaps you can say that you want to want to want him! Thus you can be very near him in your naked sincerity; and *he* will do the rest, drawing out from you longings deeper than you knew were there and pouring into you a trust and a love like that of the psalmist—whose words may soon come to your lips. Forgive me for putting this so clumsily. I am trying to say that you find you are "with God" not by achieving certain devotional exercises in his presence but by daring to be your own self as you reach towards him.

The daily time of being quietly with God becomes "adoration". And because you are with him and near him whose name is love you will have the people you care for on your heart. In this way adoration turns into "intercession", the bringing of people and needs and sorrows and joys and causes into the stream of the divine love. Be with God (adoration) with the people on your heart (intercession). It is like Aaron of old who went into the holy of holies wearing a breastplate with jewels representing the tribes of Israel whose priest he was: he went near to God with the people on his heart.

Now if the heart of the matter is seen in the daily act of quietness, the heart is no isolated organ, but a part of a whole, many-sided life of worship and action. "Being with God with the people on your heart" is the meaning of the Divine Office, of the Eucharist and of every part of your prayer and your service of the people.

The point of the Daily Office is to root your prayer in the scriptures and in the Church's corporate prayer. The Daily Office in psalm and canticle and lection tells of God's historic revelation and redemption and of the response of the Church down the ages in praise and thanksgiving. We need to soak ourselves in this if our prayer is to be fully in Christ's name and to his glory, and one with the redeemed people of God. In the Daily Office we are lifted beyond the contemporary; and let us be sure that we will serve the contemporary scene effectively only if we are sometimes lifted beyond it, praying with the Church across the ages and with the communion of God's saints. We all experience times when the Daily Office is a burden; persevere, and you find it less a burden than a wonderful liberation.

The Eucharist is the supreme way in which the people of Christ are, through our great high priest, with God with the world around on their hearts. So great is the Eucharistic mystery that it is easy for the people to miss some aspects of it. The priest will help the people to realize both the God-ward and the manward aspects of the liturgy. He will show them that it is more than their table-fellowship with one another, for it is their sharing in the worship of heaven with Blessed Mary and the Saints. He will show them that they are brought near to the awful reality of the death of the Lord on Calvary as well as to his heavenly glory. He will show them no less that here is no separated realm of piety, for the Christ upon whom they feed is one with the pains of humanity around them. As teacher and interpreter of the Eucharist, and as the one who leads the people in their sacramental worship, the priest has an immense role. But for *him*, in his own life, the Eucharist is more than that. As Christ's own minister in the words and the acts of the consecration he is drawn closer to Christ's own priesthood than words can ever tell.

You will find yourself, as celebrant at the Eucharist, privileged with a unique intensity to "be with God with the people on your heart". Do not therefore approach this act without quiet recollection before, and follow it always with quiet recollection after.

But "to be with God with the people on your heart" will be your role beyond the ordered times of prayer because it will be a part of your life. Since Bonhoeffer's influence has been felt, and his lessons have been learnt and unlearnt, and

16

since the negative concept of "religionless Christianity" has in turn given place to the more positive concept sometimes called "the new spirituality", we have been realizing how transcendence is to be found in the midst of secular experience and not apart from it, and how prayer is not only for the closet but for all the ups and downs of life. If we knew that before, or thought we did, we have been discovering it in a new vividness.

Amidst our contemporary tensions between traditional modes of prayer and the newer forms of secular spirituality, it helps greatly to recapture the simplest meaning of our Lord's high-priestly intercession: to be with God for the people. Anywhere, everywhere, God is to be found. In your daily encounters with people, God is there: you can recollect him, you can be with him, you can share your doings with him, you can shoot arrows of desire from your heart to his: and all this will be for the people's sake. You can be on the Godward side of every human situation; for the Godward side is a part of every human situation. But you are unlikely to have the power to be on the Godward side of human situations if you think that it can be done by a kind of shallow secularized activism. That is the fallacy which does so much damage at the present time. The truth is that you will have the awareness of God and the power to be on the Godward side of human situations only if you carry with you into the day's ups and downs an "interior castle" of recollection drawn from your times of quietness and eucharist and scripture. There is no by-passing the Psalmist's wisdom, "Be still and know that I am God", and there is no by-passing the example of our Lord whom Simon Peter found praying alone in a desert place a great while before day. You will not try to be wiser than the Psalmist, or wiser than our Lord.

In the coming years your prayer will not be a sort of

specialized activity. Rather will your prayer be, in a hundred ways, *you*—you with God for the people, and you with the people in God's strength. Your prayer will change much through the years, it will be free and flexible, an exciting adventure. There will be many ups and downs, times when you pray badly and times when you pray well, times when prayer is a slogging discipline and times when it is a spontaneous joy. Think of it simply as "God, myself, and the people", being with him for them, and with them for him. And the supreme fact is the prayer of Jesus himself: throughout your ministry he will be there, praying and wanting you to have a little share with him in his prayer. So tomorrow I shall ask you confidently, "Will you be diligent in prayers?", and you will answer joyfully, "I will endeavour myself so to do, the Lord being my helper".

4

PREACHING GOD TODAY

You are going to be ordained to be a minister of the gospel of God, and it will be your task and privilege to bring people to know God and to have faith in him. But we are aware that at this time there is a kind of sickness or malaise about faith in God. There is nothing new in hearing the opponents of Christianity deny God as an incredible superstition. What has been new and startling is to find within the Christian Church the various kinds of talk about the "death of God" which have been heard in recent years.

Now the phrase "the death of God" is linked with some strange philosophical and theological theories such as those of Van Büren and Altizer. I believe myself that these theories are well on the way out and already belong to past history. But the phrase "death of God" is also a symbol not of specific theories alone but of a kind of malaise or sickness of faith which has found its way within Christendom. It is about this sickness that I would speak to you now. What exactly is it? What is its cure? Can we, while we set about to cure it, try meanwhile to learn something from it?

I think that the sickness is apparent in broadly three forms.

1. There is the tendency of religious people often to picture to themselves a God who is supremely interested in the religious aspect of human life, in the religious relationship of people to himself and in all that belongs to the promotion of religious practice and culture, and is less interested in the drama of human life itself. He is the God of the temple and scarcely the God of the factory and the farm, the sciences and the technologies, and the millions as they go about working and earning. It is not true that the image of God can be seriously distorted in this way in the attitudes of devout people? I am reminded of the words of F. D. Maurice written a little over a century ago: "We have been dosing our people with religion, when what they want is not that but the living God". If this sickness has existed it is likely to have existed widely and more closely to ourselves than we who are inside the Christian tradition may be ready to see or to acknowledge. And if that is so, is it not likely also that people have been repelled by it? You remember how the prophet Jeremiah often used the word "sickness" of the *religious* state of God's people in his day, a people secure in their religious practice and yet verging on idolatry without knowing it.

2. There is the danger of our familiar imagery about God becoming dead through a lack of vigorous, imaginative response to the living truth which the imagery exists to convey. "High and lifted up", "exalted", "majestic", "almighty", "fatherly", "loving", "far", "near": those are some of the familiar phrases. But they convey the reality of God not as static tokens but as parts of a dynamic appeal to the imagination and a dynamic challenge to the mind and the conscience. Unless that dynamic appeal and challenge are conveyed again and again we may be finding the images to be like static tokens and may be understanding them in wholly inadequate ways. Thus God "high up" comes to mean God

"remote", and God's "fatherhood" becomes akin to the all too inadequate ideas of human fatherhood which an imperfect society can create.

It is not that some of the images of God are "better" than others, but that all are needed ("height" and "depth", "king" and "father"), all are inadequate, and all subserve the divine Word, living, active, sharper than a two-edged sword and piercing to the dividing of our human faculties. Without the realization of this the idea of God in our minds may be "sicklied o'er with the pale cast" of conventionalism. Is not this liable to happen? I am sure you will find many devout people for whom this has happened.

It was no doubt with these two kinds of religious malaise in mind that Professor Jenkins wrote these words:

> While most of the philosophy and theology contained in the 'Death of God' literature seems to be second-rate or worse, it is very necessary to reflect on how absolutely deadly must have been the experience which the writers of this literature must have had both in the worshipping and in the theological traditions of their Churches. For example, the God whose death is proclaimed in Thomas Altizer's *The Gospel of Christian Atheism* is a very sick God indeed. But someone must have given him this idea of God. The evidence suggests that it comes from a very sick Church.[1]

Later in the same essay Jenkins challenges us further with these words:

> God, as Christians too often appear to consider him and treat him, is just not big enough to deal with the liveliness of the world and the independence of man and is constantly in need of the support of a false authoritarianism.

[1] *Lambeth Essays on Faith* (SPCK, 1969), p. 18.

But the living God cannot be so, and is not so. It is the pressure of God's world which is now forcing the Church to have done with the mummified God . . . and to recognize that such an idol is dead beyond debate.[2]

Do these words shock you? Let them shock us into thought. Perhaps we may find that the sickness about God which is in the Church is a sickness not unto death, but a sickness whereby we may discover how to glorify God anew. (cf. John 11.4)

3. There is another kind of "death of God" malaise, very different from the foregoing. There are people with keen minds and a religious spirit whose sensitivity to the suffering widespread in the contemporary world sets them asking: Where is God, and what is God doing? We claim that God is sovereign, that the world is in his hands, that he has redeemed it by the death and resurrection of Jesus Christ. But where is he in the world today? Is he asleep? Has he gone away? Is God dead? The will to believe is there; reflection upon contemporary existence smashes it.

Here I would suggest the beginning of our answer. Recall a biblical doctrine too often forgotten, the doctrine of divine judgement. When men and nations turn away from God's laws and prefer the courses dictated by pride and selfishness to the courses dictated by conscience, calamitous results follow. God is not absent from the contemporary scene; he is present, present in judgement through the catastrophes which follow human wilfulness. And nowhere is the divine judgement as the working out of the consequences of human folly put more trenchantly than in the words of the Psalmist: "So he gave them their hearts' desire, and sent leanness withal into their souls". God is not dead, let that be our

2 ibid, p. 10.

message; God is here, here in judgement. And as the judgement of God is accepted and felt, so in the same moment may his loving kindness and mercy be found. "My song shall be of mercy and judgement", to quote the Psalmist once again. Let it however be remembered that divine judgement falls first upon God's people the Church. It was so under the old convenant, it is so under the new, for St Peter reminds us that "judgement begins at the house of God" (1 Peter 4. 17). The Church shows the message of divine judgement to the world as she sees the judgement upon herself and begins to mend her ways.

Such are three of the kinds of malaise about faith in God which have been apparent within Christendom. We are challenged by them to renew our own knowledge of the living God of the Bible. He is the God of all creation, and not the God of religion alone. He is the God for whom none of the traditional images are adequate, and all of them are necessary to convey a reality greater than themselves. He is the God who has not deserted the world, but is here in judgement.

What then will you do about all this within your own ministry? It is one thing to discuss these great themes in an academic way, but how do they bear upon our day-to-day pastoral and teaching ministry? Let me make a few practical suggestions.

1. You will remember that nothing that is human and nothing that is created lies outside the compassion of God. You will care about people for themselves, and be interested in them for themselves, and not only as potential confirmation candidates. To have a solely religious interest in people is not only to be a bad pastor, it is also to be turning the true

God into a sickly caricature of himself. Similarly, be concerned about the tremendous issues of the world we live in: poverty, affluence, pollution, race, war, violence, revolution. It is not that you will know the solution of these matters, or will make them the stock in trade of your preaching. It is rather that by your concern you will be sensitive to God's own concern, and so your thought about God will be nearer to the truth of his righteousness as a faithful creator. Through our concern about the world in which God is present in judgement and in mercy we learn to be in touch with the true God when we meet God in the Church and in the sacraments.

2. In using the historic imagery about God, imagery which is likely always to be with us, be very tender towards the simple, unquestioning piety of those who picture, believe, pray, and ask no questions. But with that tenderness combine a readiness to be often asking, gently of others and severely of oneself, "What are we really saying?", "What do we really mean?" It is in the asking and the answering that faith becomes lively. To say that God is high above us is to say that we depend upon him as our creator, and that his holiness is beyond compare. And in what sense is God our Father? To let it be thought that he is just like your father or my father may cause more misunderstanding than light. It is the complacent failure of the Christian teacher to ask these questions which can allow people to drift into a faith which seems secure but is really rather sick. I am sure too that, in talking with those who are not professed theists and yet are friendly and questioning, it is well sometimes to start not at our end but at theirs. If a man does not say "God", what does he say? What are those values or imperatives or absolutes, within him and beyond, which signify most for him? It sometimes happens that such a discussion may reach a point

where one is saying: "That is how you speak; it is not far from what we Christians mean by *God* or by *grace*".

3. The recovery of the doctrine of the divine judgement about which I was speaking is a direct appeal to biblical truth. But let the appeal be to the whole of the biblical concept, adumbrated in the Psalms and maturely gathered up in St John. The supreme act of the divine judgement is the coming of Christ: "and this is the judgement, that the light is come into the world, and men loved the darkness rather than the light for their deeds were evil". It must be in the figure of Jesus crucified and risen that we present the divine judgement and the divine mercy. I see no other way of bringing the themes of sovereignty, power, compassion, judgement, home to our contemporaries except in terms of Jesus in whom these divine actions are focused. On another occasion I shall be speaking to you about "Preaching Jesus Today" with these thoughts in mind.

Let me add one final counsel. *Beware of attitudes which try to make God smaller than the God who has revealed himself to us in Jesus.* Let me illustrate what I mean.

Whenever exponents of the Christian faith treat it as something which we have to "defend" like a beleagured fortress or a fragile structure they are making God to be smaller than he is. (*a*) There is the idea that the greatness of the God of the Bible is protected by a kind of defensive literalism which insists on the historicity of the narratives and supposes that to waver on the Mosaic authorship of the Pentateuch or the sojourn of Jonah in the whale is to make grievous concessions to modern secularism. But the God of the Bible is majestic enough not to require such protection, as he is able to use in his scriptures not only literal history but poetry, drama, myth, and symbol also in conveying his truth to mankind. (*b*) There is a kind of defensive Catholicism which supposes that no risks must be taken in the process of Christian unity, as if Catholic truth needed "protecting", whereas the gifts of God are powerful enough to vindicate themselves in the growing together of different traditions. The truth of God is greater than our efforts to conserve it. (*c*) So too there is a spirit of fearfulness which thinks that no good can ever come of movements which are outside the camp of Christendom, forgetting that God could use a Cyrus, an Assyria, or an altar-to-an-unknown-deity in his great purpose in history. We are not indeed to confuse what God does as redeemer in the unique sphere of gospel and Church with what he does as illuminator through the light that lighteth every man; but to be blind to the latter is not to enhance the former or to understand it better. (*d*) One more instance. There are those who, eager to respect the contemporary mind and the claims of reason, try to deny to God anything which seems to be beyond the contemporary grasp or rational apprehension. To do this is to miss that God's thoughts are not our thoughts nor God's ways our ways, and that eye has not seen, ear has not heard, nor has it entered into the heart of man to conceive what God has prepared for them that love him. Such is the God whom we preach, and man's need for him today is as desperate as it ever was.

5

PREACHING JESUS TODAY

I

Jesus Christ is himself the gospel which we preach (cf. Acts 5.42, 8.25, 11.20). He is himself the essence of the good news. I ask you to think about some of the formidable difficulties which confront us today as we set about the preaching of Jesus. I am not thinking only of our sermons, which are almost always addressed to those who are within the circle of faith, but of all that the Church does to convey a message about Jesus, a message whose heart and centre is Jesus.

There is first of all the difficulty of conveying a historical faith to people who, like so many of our contemporaries, are without any sense of history. True, we preach Jesus as living and contemporary, and we link the past history with his presence now in the Eucharist. Yet our understanding of his character and message is derived from historical events which occurred nearly two thousand years ago. True, we say that God is living and active in the world today; yet we ascribe unique and revelatory importance to those things which we say God wrought through Jesus on the soil of Palestine in the time of Pontius Pilate. However contemporary we may try to be, our authority rests upon an "old, old story". And all this amidst a generation for whom the sense of the past is very faint. I would say that one of the biggest differences between the up-and-coming generation in England and its predecessors is that it has a thick curtain between itself and past history or tradition. My own generation felt itself to belong to a stream which flowed through past time: this generation has its consciousness filled and absorbed by the present. The "secular" outlook, as we call it, means largely an outlook limited by the frontiers of the present "saeculum".

Furthermore, where people *are* ready to be interested in the past they look at it with a more critical eye about its credibility, and it is felt that the history of Jesus of Nazareth is unsure. The impact of Form-Criticism has undermined the view that the Gospels can be read as diary-reminiscences and has set them in the context of the preaching, the worship, and the theologizing of the early Church. Now we can say, and for my own part I do not hesitate to say, that the Form-critical method need not involve historical scepticism. If the Gospels give us interpretative portraits of Jesus painted within the post-Resurrection Church the picture conveyed may be a true one if the interpretations are true, and we are shown Jesus as he was in his total impact upon his followers. We may be no less sure that it was not the Church or the evangelists who created Jesus but Jesus who created them.

Yet while we may ourselves feel assured about the sufficient historical basis of the gospel, there remains a feeling of remoteness between the Gospels and the world in which people live today. Take the Synoptic Gospels. The narratives are full of miraculous happenings. We can expound and defend these in the context of the Incarnation, and for my part I do not hesitate to do so. But our hearers may feel: "They may be true, but is this the world we live in?" And the teaching is full of apocalyptic imagery; and to say that this of course needs interpretation and is not to be taken literally is to emphasize again the gap between the world of the Gospels and the world of today. Fewer people today have the poetic feeling which builds an imaginative bridge from one culture to another. Because of the remoteness of the world view of the synoptists many modern readers more easily feel the timeless appeal of Jesus in the "universal" imagery of the Fourth Gospel: life, light, bread, water, door, way, truth, word; and the Johannine discourses reach across the centuries. But here too the problems of history raise their head.

II

Let me now suggest to you a way of approaching the problem of presenting Jesus Christ to our contemporaries. We start with those facts about him which very few would wish to deny.

First, Jesus of Nazareth, a prophet and a teacher, did exist. We can safely say that to deny this is a piece of historical eccentricity.

Next, Jesus of Nazareth died by crucifixion. Here too we are on unassailable ground.

Then, as a result of the career of Jesus of Nazareth there came into history the phenomenon of Christianity, the new movement with its society, its teaching, its rites, its doctrine, its ethics, its impact on the world for better or for worse. This is again indisputable, whatever significance is ascribed to it and in whatever way the causal connection between Jesus and the Church is traced.

So far we are on agreed ground. Now I take a further step and ask about the new phenomenon of Christianity and its character. Within this new phenomenon of Christianity there is a strikingly new valuation of *suffering*. This is seen in the teachings, the liturgies, the ethical attitudes, the view of the world and the practical behaviour of the Christians. The ignominious death by crucifixion which was meted out to Jesus is not shame and disgrace: it is "good news", it is of God, it has a victorious character. And for the Christians to suffer is not defeat or tragedy; it has a like victorious character. They are "glad to be counted worthy to suffer dishonour for the name" (Acts 5.41). They are in the midst of sufferings "more than conquerors" (Rom. 8.37).

This new valuation of suffering, which recurs again and again in the apostolic teaching and in the history of the Christian mission, is not a cult of martyrdom or a kind of masochism or a laudation of suffering in itself. It goes with a belief in a divine use of suffering which links it creatively with sacrificial love and with a self-fulfilment within it and beyond it. It goes with a conviction about the suffering of Jesus as not ignominious but creative in its impact.

Now we ask: If this be a significant part of the phenomenon of Christianity, what happened to bring it about? It is true that Jesus gave to his disciples a good deal of teaching about the meaning of his coming suffering and death, but this teaching did not apparently penetrate their minds. It baffled them, and when Jesus died the disciples had not learnt the secret; indeed the secret died with him. Something *happened* to create for the disciples the new doctrine of the death as significant and victorious. I believe that the something which happened was the Resurrection. The alternative theories, that the apostles were deceived or deceiving, or the victims of hallucination or wishful thinking, seem to me to call for an extreme kind of credulity, a

30

credulity far removed from scientific history. I believe that there was an event, and that the apostles were right in their belief about it. Jesus had been raised from death.

We have often heard discussions about the sense in which the Resurrection was "bodily" or "spiritual", and our understanding of those categories is far from adequate. I see as a very important characteristic of the Resurrection, both in the Gospel narratives and in the apostles' teaching, that it was the Resurrection of *the crucified one*: it was the coming back to the disciples, and the making available to future generations, of *Jesus who died, Jesus in his death*. It is not that the death is an incident now left behind: no, the death is always with us, vindicated in its undying significance. Not for nothing are the episodes in the Gospel traditions where the wounds of the crucifixion are still visible when the risen Jesus appears. The risen Jesus is still the crucified one.

Here then is the central point of the history of Jesus. He was not a forgotten crucified teacher. His impact survived, and Christianity came into existence because the Resurrection happened and because it was the Resurrection of the crucified. And besides being the events which brought Christianity to birth the Death and Resurrection are the events which characterize the nature of Christianity. It is a gospel of life through death, of losing life so as to find it. Thus the Christian's act of allegiance to the risen Lord Jesus was, and still is, an act of acceptance of the way of the Cross. So too the act of faith in the Christian God is an act which sees the sacrifice of self right down to the point of death and destruction, and then says: This, and only this, is the sovereign power of God. In the imagery of the Apocalypse the lamb (self-sacrifice) and the throne (sovereignty) go together.

Crucifixion-Resurrection was the core of the history with which the early Church was concerned: it was this which was the centre of the preaching and the liturgy. But here was no mere mystery-religion of a dying and rising deity, for in the case of Jesus it mattered greatly who and of what sort was the Man who thus died and rose again. How had he lived? What did he do, and what did he teach? So besides the story of Good Friday and Easter the Church treasured the traditions about the words and the works of Jesus, and these traditions eventually came to be embodied in the written Gospels.

III

Such is the approach to the history of Jesus which I suggest to you. I start with the very few data: that the history of Jesus was such as to account for the strikingly new and creative element in primitive Christianity. This gives the Death and the Resurrection as the central facts, and also as the heart of the interpretation of Jesus. Like Bultmann I see the act of faith in the risen Lord as faith in the supremacy of the Cross: unlike him I am convinced that the Resurrection was a historic event, acceptable on strong evidence, which gave to the Cross its significance for the apostles. Unlike him also I believe that the early Church was greatly interested in the life and teaching of Jesus for its own sake, always in the light of the central Cross and Resurrection faith.

I suggest to you that as the Cross and the Resurrection were the spearhead of the gospel's relevance and potency in the first century so they can be also for our contemporary world. Ours is a world full of suffering and frustration: of what significance to it is Jesus who lived and died nearly two thousand years ago? The answer is: chiefly in this, that in the Death and Resurrection he shows not only the way for man but the very image of God himself. Is there within or beyond our suffering and frustrated universe any purpose, way, meaning, sovereignty? We answer, yes, there is purpose, way, meaning, sovereignty, and the Death and Resurrection of Jesus portray it as living through dying, as losing self to find self, as the power of sacrificial love. To commit oneself to this way is to be near to the secret of God's own sovereignty, near to the power which already wins victories over evil and will ultimately prevail. That is the point at which Jesus can be shown to be near to our own world; and when he is found to be near at this point then his life and teaching are found to have their compelling fascination. Through the life and the teaching there runs the principle "he who exalts himself shall be abased, and he who humbles himself shall be exalted". Through the life and teaching there is the strange blending of authority and humility.

So the Church is called to be the fellowship of Christ crucified and risen. In the Eucharist it proclaims Christ's death and feeds upon his life. We are familiar with this; but how tremendous are the implications. It implies a fellowship of Christians marked by an unselfish openness to one another in Christ's name, a like openness in the service of the community and a commitment to the way which led to Calvary. There are those who wonder whether the old institutional Church can rise to this, its essential calling and there are those who are finding the Cross-Resurrection commitment in ways outside the old institutions.

Here however is, I suggest, the point of impact of the old story of Jesus upon our new world: *die to live*. Here too is the meaning of the Church, and the meaning of apostolic ministry: "always bearing about in the body the dying of Jesus, that the life also of Jesus may be manifested in our body" (2 Cor. 4.10).

6

THE PRIEST AND POLITICS

I wish to speak to you about the Priest and Politics, meaning by Politics those affairs of State and society with which the Christian Church is inevitably involved. The problem of the Priest and Politics has been prominent through the centuries as the affairs of Church and State have clashed or intermingled. I have only to recall the names of a few of my own predecessors, Becket, Cranmer, Laud, William Temple, to see both that the problem of the Priest and Politics is unavoidable and that it takes different forms in different ages. Your own ministry is going to be exercised at a time when certain social issues are raising their heads with new and intense force—race, poverty, the third world, violence, pollution—and unless Christianity is to recede into a vacuum it has much to say to these problems and they have much to say to it.

Let me start by describing two possible roles which a priest might adopt and sometimes does adopt, roles which are likely to strike you as profoundly lopsided or unsatisfactory. If we are dissatisfied with both of them we may then explore a more excellent way.

Here is a priest who is deeply imbued with the priority of the spiritual and the integrity of the gospel. He preaches the gospel of salvation by faith in Christ crucified, and he dwells upon the conversion of individuals to personal conviction. He reasons of righteousness and judgement to come, and men and women are led to repent and believe. What are the sins of which they repent? Pride, uncharitableness, greed, selfishness, inchastity. The second great commandment is linked inextricably with the first, and people are led by their conversion to lives of practical service to their neighbours. Yet both the evangelist and the converts can be in blinkers about parts of the intimate environment in which their Christian commitment must be lived out. My own experience covers many different places in the world. I recall congregations of white Christians who would be antagonized by the presence of black Christians worshipping with them. I recall congregations who are unaware that any questions of Christian conscience are posed by their enjoyment of a very high standard of comfort not far from places of desperate poverty and squalor. But it is about the priest that we are thinking specially, and both these illustrations may imply a priest who is blithely unaware that anything is amiss so long as souls are "converted" and "saved". "You see the gospel must always come first." Is it surprising that in some quarters there grows a seething discontent with both Christianity and the Church? Men ask "Converted to what?", "Saved for what?"

Now another priest. He takes the words of the Magnificat in deadly earnest. He knows that racial discrimination is blasphemy, that poverty and hunger have something urgently to do with Christianity, that if violence is possible in a "just war" it may be no less possible in a "just revolution", that courage is a better guide than caution—"we must stand up and be counted". So his time is spent in the organizing of protests and campaigns, in leading the people in demonstrations for the causes which fire him, as well as in generous philanthropic actions; and the themes of his sermons are race, poverty, and war. But how large can be the defects of such a ministry. The people can be stirred into protests about the misdeeds of others in their own and other countries, and they are not always helped to discover and repent of their own sins. Nor are they being helped to the knowledge and love of God, the way of holiness and the hope of heaven. The concentration on particular issues misses the perspective of the great truths of God and Man. When causes and opinions are substituted for God, prayer, and repentance the outcome can be bitterness and shallowness no less than love and service.

Both these pictures of a priest are, I acknowledge, rather a caricature. But if they are exaggerated enough for posing the issues sharply, I think they are also near enough to the bone for touching your thoughts about your own ministry. I ask now: have we some guidelines towards a better way than those which I have just been pillorying?

1. First, let us agree that the first priority is to preach the gospel to men and women so that they may be converted to our Lord. But if a person is to be truly converted the conversion must embrace all his personal and social relationships. He does not exist in a vacuum. He is a man, a creature in God's own image; he is a husband, a father, an uncle, a neighbour, an employer or a manager or a workman, a citizen; he has amusements, hobbies, leisure, money, income, savings, health or sickness, power or impotence, wealth or poverty. Convert him, you say. So be it, but the Christ to whom you convert him wants the whole of him. When Paul and Silas were in prison at Philippi and there was an earthquake and they were liberated and the jailer was

converted and, with his whole household, baptized, it was a *jailer* who was converted, not a man in a vacuum; and we would hope that as a Christian jailer he was a different person in his dealings with people and with his job. I suggest that there are three broadly contrasted procedures. It is possible to preach the gospel of conversion without any sight of its social context. It is possible to preach a social gospel which omits the reality of conversion to Christ. Be it your wisdom to preach the gospel of conversion, making it clear that it is the whole man with all his relationships who is converted to Jesus as the Lord of all he is and does.

2. It follows that through its concern with the context of human lives the Church of God is bound to make judgements about what is right and wrong in human relationships in society. No doubt this is part of the "binding and loosing" with which our Lord charged the apostles. But how do we know what to teach about human relationships? There is, I believe, a great tradition of Christian teaching about main principles drawn from our Lord and the apostles, calling for interpretation and application in changing circumstances and yet constant in its main lines. Thus, to give a few instances, the selfish motive in all affairs is always wrong, and the altruistic motive is always right. Wealth is always dangerous to its possessor, and the rich man can only with difficulty be saved. There is no discrimination between races in God's eyes, and there must be no discrimination in man's eyes; and different races share freely in the Church's fellowship. Some of the basic Christian principles I would describe as pre-political rather than as political. For instance, I do not think it can be said that democracy or majority rule as such is a Christian principle; and we remember that Christ sometimes showed contempt for the views of majorities. What is however a Christian principle is the equal right of

every person created in God's image to the full realization of his powers of mind and body, and this includes full and free citizenship with democracy as a corollary. We should always distinguish carefully a non-Christian conception of the rights of people to do what they like, and a Christian conception of their right to become by God's grace their own truest selves. In this way Christianity both endorses, and criticizes and corrects, the ideal of democracy.

3. How then are these and other Christian judgements by the Church to be enunciated and applied? It seems to me that a variety of *media* come into view. There are matters which should be so much the stuff of ordinary Christian conviction that Christian people influence society in respect of them by every sort of witness and pressure. There are matters on which the Church's leaders in their teaching role must declare the main principles with enough specific illustration or parable to be relevant and intelligible. Then there are prophets, who can never be organized or appointed, for they are raised up by God as he wills, to declare, like Israel's prophets of old, their perceptions of the wickedness of states or nations and the divine judgement upon them. Amos was a shepherd and a dresser of sycamore trees, and God called him to prophesy against his people. The spirit blows where he wills. "Would that all the Lord's people were prophets" said Moses (Num. 11.29). "And *some* prophets" said St Paul (Eph. 4.11).

But certain distinctions can be drawn. It is one thing to state main Christian principles, or to denounce a particular downright evil. It is another thing to commend a particular programme, on which the technical skills and wisdom of competent Christians may differ, and to say "This is *the* Christian programme", as if to unchurch or label as second-grade any Christians who might for good reasons dissent.

Here I would recall the guidance given by Archbishop William Temple who did perhaps more than any other English churchman to direct the Christian influence in the political and social field in the present century. His book *Christianity and the Social Order* was published in 1941. This book has been much criticized for its advocacy of views about the banking system which the critics held to be technically unsound. But these views were included in an Appendix setting out what Temple called a Programme; and Temple was careful to say that, whereas the Principles in the body of the book were in his judgement essentially Christian and called for proclamation by the whole Church, the Programme was a purely personal set of proposals for which he would not claim any similar endorsement or authority. This distinction is important. So too is another distinction which Temple drew in the same book, between the role of the Church in teaching principles in its pronouncements and the role of Christian citizens, inspired by those principles, in carrying them unselfconsciously with their own skill and wisdom into public affairs, in national and local government, in industry and commerce, and in every field of life open to them.

4. In bearing its witness in this manner in the political and social realms the Church will see every part of its mission in the total perspective of the reconciliation of mankind to God and of heaven as the goal for every man and woman made in the divine image. This grasp of the total perspective will prevent us from substituting the denunciation of the misdeeds of other communities for our own repentance and our own response to the way of holiness. It will no less prevent us from giving absolute and final significance to causes or policies which may be only small fragments within the ultimate range of the Kingdom of God. It will prevent us

also from allowing our concern for physical suffering and material welfare to diminish our concern for the eternal life in another world which is the destiny of every man or woman who does not forfeit it. It is good to recall the story of the great Anglican divine Richard Hooker when he lay dying. They asked him what he was thinking about, and he replied "the number of angels and the excellence of their order, joying that it was so in heaven and would that it might be so on earth". Our concern as Christians, and no less as priests, is with a divine order embracing heaven and earth, and with its reflection in every part of human affairs. That is the true context of our witness within the social scene. Our otherworldly calling tells us of the goal and helps us not to lose heart or lose patience as we witness to justice and brotherhood and human dignity in the community where we are.

If these are some broad principles to guide us, what counsels have I in particular for you who are to be priests at a time when these questions press themselves urgently and even violently upon us? I claim no oracular authority, but I speak from an experience of public affairs which has been fairly stormy, and I know how hard it is to be sure whether one is saying too much or too little, or being too timid or too rash. From my own tangle of experience I will dare to give you this advice.

1. Be aware of the new and powerful trends in the world which bear upon the Church and its mission. A country or a town or a village may feel itself to be peaceful and secure, and upheavals of one kind or another can be very near. I have, for instance, seen our sister Anglican Church in the United States in one decade feel utterly secure in its prosperity and in the apparent impregnability of the "American way of

life", and in the next decade convulsed by the onset of violent social upheavals. Notice also the new role which the race problem is assuming in many parts of the world. To my generation with its old-fashioned liberalism the race problem meant getting white people and black people to be kind to one another. To your generation the race problem often means the seething unrest of black people who will tolerate white domination no longer, and who ask why if it was right for us white people in Europe to fight for liberation from Hitler it is wrong for them to fight for liberation from their oppressors. It is in such a world that you will be ministering, and one part of it has repercussions upon another. And even when a particular problem or tragedy does not seem immediately to come your way remember your fellow Christians for whom it does, and see your ministry as a part of the Church's witness in every place.

2. Take your share in the task of Christian people to study together and form right judgements based on knowledge and Christian insight. I am thinking of such issues as industrial relations, and third world in its relation to our world, war and violence, obscenity and censorship, race relations. It may often be for you as priests to rouse the laity to think responsibly about these questions, but when they are aroused you will find that they have knowledge which you have not and you will be learning from them in a partnership of Christian concern. That is how the mind of the Church is to be formed.

3. Help your congregation to be a caring congregation, active in its service of some human need or distress. But always let the caring for human need be linked with the caring for God himself and the winning of lives to him. Never let your leadership in social causes weaken your

pastoral ministry to your own people. There is a world of difference between the priest who compensates for pastoral failure with his own people by an embittered advocacy of public causes and the priest whose power of public prophecy is drawn from the hard school of personal pastoral experience.

4. Amidst the vast scene of the world's problems and tragedies you may feel that your own ministry seems so small, so insignificant, so concerned with the trivial. What a tiny difference it can make to the world that you should run a youth club, or preach to a few people in a church, or visit families with seemingly small result. But consider: the glory of Christianity is its claim that small things really matter and that the small company, the very few, the one man, the one woman, the one child are of infinite worth to God. Let that be your inspiration. Consider our Lord himself. Amidst a vast world with its vast empires and vast events and tragedies our Lord devoted himself to a small country, to small things and to individual men and women, often giving hours of time to the very few or to the one man or woman. In a country where there were movements and causes which excited the allegiance of many—the Pharisees, the Zealots, the Essenes, and others—our Lord gives many hours to one woman of Samaria, one Nicodemus, one Martha, one Mary, one Lazarus, one Simon Peter, for the infinite worth of the one is the key to the Christian understanding of the many.

It is to a ministry like that of our Lord himself that you are called. The Gospel you preach affects the salvation of the world, and you may help your people to influence the world's problems. But you will never be nearer to Christ than in caring for the one man, the one woman, the one child. His authority will be given to you as you do this, and his joy will be yours as well.

7

THE PRIEST AS ABSOLVER

I wish to consider with you Confession and Absolution in
relation to our ministry as priests and to our lives as Christians. We are charged both to preach a gospel of divine
forgiveness and to be ready to hear the confessions of
individuals and to give them "the benefit of absolution".
How shall we lead the people in these things unless we are
men who have faced deeply the realities of sin and divine
forgiveness in ourselves?

I

We are pledged as priests of the Church of England to be
ready for a ministry described thus in the Exhortation in the
Order for Holy Communion:

> And because it is requisite, that no man should come to
> the Holy Communion but with a full trust in God's
> mercy and with a good conscience: therefore if there be
> any of you who by this means cannot quiet his own

conscience therein but requireth further comfort or counsel, let him come to me or to some other discreet and learned minister of God's word, and open his grief; that by the ministry of God's holy word he may receive the benefit of absolution, together with ghostly counsel and advice, to the quieting of his conscience and the avoiding of all scruple and doubtfulness.

The Order for the Visitation of the Sick is more explicit. The rubric directs:

Here shall the sick person be moved to make a special confession of his sins, if he feels his conscience troubled with any weighty matter.

And the priest is then instructed "to absolve him (if he humbly and heartily desire it) after the following manner", and the formula for him to use is provided:

Our Lord Jesus Christ, who hath left power to his Church to absolve all sinners who truly repent and believe in him; of his great mercy forgive thee thine offences. And by his authority committed to me I absolve thee from all thy sins, in the name of the Father, and of the Son, and of the Holy Ghost.

It seems reasonable for us to suppose that as this is the only formula for "the benefit of absolution" which the Prayer Book includes it is right for us to use it whenever we minister that "benefit" to an individual penitent. In the Ordinal the inclusion of the words "whose sins thou dost forgive they are forgiven and whose sins thou dost retain they are retained" in the formula of ordination (a feature peculiar to the Anglican rite) was no doubt intended to emphasize the ministry of absolution, though scholarly exegesis of John 20.22 gives the words a wider reference.

It is noteworthy that the proposed Anglican-Methodist Ordinal enhances the prominence of the ministry of reconciliation. Within the Examination of the Candidates the bishop charges them "to call sinners to repentance" and more specifically "to absolve the penitent". And in the prayer that follows the laying on of hands he asks God to "strengthen them to proclaim effectually the gospel of thy salvation, and to declare to the penitent the absolution and remission of their sins".

Preaching the gospel of divine reconciliation, declaring the absolution of sinners in the public services, ministering absolution to individual penitents when asked to do so: we have indeed a ministry in which the tremendous issue of sin and forgiveness stands out in prominence. And the advance of Christian unity will not lessen this. We dare not consider our public office apart from our own spiritual need and the divine judgement upon ourselves.

> Moses and Aaron among his priests, and Samuel among such as call upon his name: these called upon the Lord, and he heard them.
> He spake unto them out of the cloudy pillar: for they kept his testimonies, and the law that he gave them.
> Thou heardest them, O Lord our God: thou forgavest them, O God, and punishedst their own inventions.
> O magnify the Lord our God, and worship him upon his holy hill: for the Lord our God is holy.

(Psalm 99.6–9)

II

Through the centuries in which the Prayer Book has been in use there has been amongst Anglicans a tradition of the voluntary use of Confession and Absolution. Let me describe its rationale as it has come to be practised and understood.

The voluntary nature of private confession is emphasized. Whereas the Church of Rome has appeared to teach that the Sacrament of Penance is necessary in the case of mortal sin, our Church has insisted that we are free to confess our sins to God alone without the hearing of a priest; and if we do this in sincerity God's forgiveness is sure. But our Church has no less insisted that we are free to confess in the sacramental way if we so desire and to ask absolution from the priest. The motives which have led people to this course have been powerful indeed. There is the feeling that thoroughness is called for in our confession, and the sacramental way certainly ensures this. There is the feeling that some painful and costly act on our part is not amiss in the confession of sins which wound the heart of our Lord. There is the feeling that the corporate nature of the Church makes appropriate an acknowledgement of our sins to "the family" of which the priest is representative. Finally, the word of absolution has a salutary decisiveness, blending Word and Act in a truly evangelical way.

Understood in this way, the practice of "going to confession", which had always had its place within the spectrum of Anglican piety, was powerfully revived by the Oxford Movement and increased greatly amongst Anglicans in the early and middle years of the present century. In an earlier phase it had been sometimes regarded as a mark of a "party" to go to confession, one of the characteristics of the "good Catholic" as distinct from the shallow ritualist. But increasingly the use of confession spread amongst Anglicans irrespective of parties or schools of thought, being valued on its merits as a path of spirituality which any were free to choose. Besides the queues of penitents before the great festivals at the well-known Anglo-Catholic shrines there have been men and women in many diverse places drawn to confession whether regularly or occasionally. Confessors have drawn freely upon varieties of spiritual writers, Anglican, Roman, and other, for training in guidance and direction; and there has persisted what may fairly be called an Anglican tradition of spiritual direction which seeks to hint and suggest ways of advance rather than to dominate or control, and sees the priest's role more as that of a physician than that of a judge. Protestant critics of sacramental confession as an intrusion between the Christian and his Saviour have failed to realize how the practice can bring a Christian vividly near to Christ crucified.

While Anglicans have shrunk from defining a distinction between mortal and venial sins, there has been in their practice a broad correspondence with the two concepts known to Roman moralists as "confessions of obligation" and "confessions of devotion". There is the use of confession by the soul in desperate need, as in the case of scandalous sin or at the time of a deep conversion or a return after a lapse from Christian practice. There is also the use of confession by those who are trying to follow the call to holiness and accept the humiliation of confession as a help along the way. As for the term "mortal" sin who knows whether the pride or complacency of the devout may not be as deadly as the scandalous acts of the profligate? Experience shows that we need to confess not only the grievous lapses which worry our conscience but our whole condition of failure in all its symptoms so that all may be disclosed and cleansed in the divine light. The light of absolution will then penetrate the entire self.

III

Today, however, the signs of a time of erosion or decline in the use of confession are apparent. Both in the Church of Rome and in the Church of England similar signs of a decrease are reported, and the confessionals are no longer thronged as in the past. While there are many who still practice Confession, the "regular" use which was familiar in many parishes is considerably less. As might be expected, a host of reasons for this can be given. There has been, alas, a lamentable decline in the sense of sin, the longing for forgiveness, the grasp of the realities of guilt, judgement, and mercy. The failure to confess is in line with the failure to pray. Yet as in other parts of the contemporary religious predicament we have to ask whether there are also trends which are salutary and creative amidst much which is merely negative. I would try to draw out some of the factors which seem significant.

1. There has been a big growth in other agencies for bringing relief to people in their personal troubles. Amidst the strains of modern life these troubles often take the form of deep psychological disturbance. Skills are needed here which the priest is not usually trained to possess. Furthermore, those who are led to see themselves as patients to be healed are less ready to see themselves as sinners to be forgiven.

2. There is the growing social sense, in religion as in other parts of life, which finds the old confessional unduly individualistic. True, the priest represents the Church, and absolution is in the Church's name and in the Church's bosom. Yet while it was the social sense of the Church which in Tractarian times revived the ministry of absolution, it is a different kind of social sense which has now come to be

dissatisfied with the Tractarian form of it. Sin is not only the sin of me and the sin of you and the sin of him and the sin of her, for the failings of us all are bound together, or so it seems to those who think in terms of a social penitence. Hence comes the feeling that a different technique is called for if we are to hold together the "power of the keys" and the "confess your sins one to another" of St James. In the Roman Catholic Church in some places the sense of the corporateness of sin and forgiveness has been finding expression in new liturgical methods. There have been services in which a collective self-examination by the congregation is followed by visits of the participants to the confessionals to be followed in turn by a united thanksgiving for God's forgiveness. It seems likely that these trends in "penitential liturgy" will grow. So too may a recovered seriousness in the congregational confession and absolution in the Anglican liturgy.

3. There is also an awareness that the spirituality fostered by sacramental confession in the past may be defective in the range of its ethical content. There can be penitents who may accuse themselves of the more obvious violations of humility or charity and yet may wear undisturbed blinkers about, for example, their attitudes on race or their prejudices on issues of public righteousness. Perhaps this is a criticism less of confession and absolution as such than of weaknesses in the general character of Church life and religious practice.

4. There is amongst young people an openness of unselfconscious personal relationships which shies at the impersonality of sacramental confession as hitherto practised. In the past this impersonality of the sacramental procedure has been felt to be immensely valuable: it shows that you are not having a conversation with Father X but confessing your

49

sins to God. It enhances the self-effacement of the priest, whose personal counsels are subordinated to the sacramental act. How often has the advice been given and gratefully acted upon: "Think of our Lord and you will not be afraid; do not think about the priest, he is only there to act in our Lord's name". Today, however, we are sometimes told that this sacramental impersonality is less helpful; it is in the openness of a more personal relationship to the priest that the sacramental act has its context. This is in part, I think, the difference between generations, and in part the spread of a more "existentialist" outlook in religion.

So the turmoil of our time confronts us both with a sad and deadly weakening of the grasp of sin and divine forgiveness, reflected in sacramental as well as in evangelistic life, and also with the pressure of new ideas of which some at least may prove to be creative. What then of ourselves? It is easy for us, if we will, to cling to the old ways and to dismiss every one of the new trends as modern wilfulness. Or it is easy for us to lose our hold upon the great realities about sin and divine forgiveness on the ground that there are new ideas for us to attend to. The one way is the way of an obscurantism which can give us the gospel in a vacuum. The other way is the way of a secularizing erosion. Neither is the right way for the man of God in any age.

IV

My counsel to you is to study and learn from every one of the new trends and critiques which I have mentioned, but to do so with the historic gospel in your heart. Let the use of psychological methods be such as does not supplant but rather enlarges the conscious area of moral responsibility. Let the enhanced awareness of the sin of society lead the individual to see not less but more clearly in Christ's light that his sin is his own sin. I would plead for a deep and wide recovery of *Repentance* in its biblical meaning.

To repent is to turn, ἐπιστρέφειν, and to have a change of mind, μετανοεῖν. The turning and the change of mind are God's gift, and they are a turning and a change of mind towards God. We begin with a glimpse of the vision of God in his power and wonder and beauty and goodness. We praise him for his greatness as creator, for his mercy as redeemer and for his continuing lovingkindness to ourselves. And a central point within this vision is the Cross of Calvary where Christ died for us. In the turning towards him and the change of our mind towards him there come the realization of our littleness and insignificance as his creatures, the absurdity of our pride and selfishness and fear, the shame of our ingratitude. We see ourselves in his light, exposing every corner of our being to him. We grieve bitterly, and we rejoice in the truth. But we are sinners, and we cannot climb up again by our own act. Impotent, undeserving, we await *his* act, the *absolvo te*.

It is in terms of the biblical truth of repentance in its depth and breadth that you will do your work as preacher, as absolver and as counsellor, and will see yourself as a penitent in God's presence.

As absolver try to bring as much care and reality as you can into the confessions and absolutions within the church services. There is room here for a big work of renewal and reconstruction. Be ready for the ministry of private confession and absolution with a technical grasp of it, whether or not its use is frequent in the parish where you minister. Know the usual forms for beginning and ending a confession which the penitent will use, in case he stumbles and needs to be helped. Know that the penitent may not desire a sermonette from you, but may welcome a few words of incisive and tender counsel before the absolution. Know how to say the absolution quietly and decisively: it is not a conversation-piece of yours but a sacramental Word and Act. Know that it helps if you are calm, serene, and in the true sense "business-like". I know of the pain which is caused by amateurish bungling: "he talked and talked and talked, and I was not sure whether he gave me an absolution or not".

Training for the giving of counsel is a vast subject. Some priests will be thoroughly trained for a specialized ministry of counselling of a psychiatric kind. Every priest should know enough of psychology to realize how little he knows, and to recognize those instances where he should advise recourse to a psychiatrist. But there are the many occasions where the priest can help the penitent by his knowledge of spirituality together with practical wisdom and sympathy. Above all, it will be your role to help people to grasp that dimension of sin and divine forgiveness which a purely clinical approach can easily ignore. Help people to know that there is joy in heaven over one sinner who repents. Help them to be sensitive to God's will, and to have his glory as their motive and their goal.

Besides your ministry there is *you*; and the grasp upon you of these realities whose preacher and steward you will be. You will try to find what is the will of God about the way you shall confess your own sins, bearing in mind the liberties which our Church sets before us.

Many find that the significance of sacramental confession for them may change through the passing of time. A first confession may be an occasion of vivid realization of the Cross and a decisive turning-point in spiritual depth. Subsequent confessions in the early years can have a like vividness. Then a time may come when the vividness fades and confession seems to have the staleness of a humdrum discipline. So there comes the tendency to say "why bother?", and amidst the intense busyness and tiredness of work to let both self-examination and confession slip. It is, however, when going to confession requires a sheer discipline of the will that a new and creative aspect of it may begin to emerge: the act of the will in confessing may enable you to escape vagueness and drift and to regain a true picture of yourself. Then you may find in new ways how the lovingkindness of God can hide, as it were, beneath the recesses of your failure, and you are humbled by discovering how God can use you in spite of yourself. Your humility and your grateful trust in him are renewed, and the joy of priesthood revives for the good of your work and your people.

8

CHRIST'S DOCTRINE AND DISCIPLINE

I am sure you have many times read and pondered the questions which the bishop will put to you in the Ordination Service. I ask you now to notice that there are two or three which mention specifically the person of our Lord and bring out the way in which your ordination involves a close relationship to him. Both the deacon-to-be and the priest-to-be are asked if they are truly called "by the will of our Lord": it is Jesus Christ who calls you. Both again are asked whether they will base their lives and the lives of their families upon Christ's teaching. These pledges bring you very near to Christ himself. And there is a further question which mentions Christ in a striking way that I specially want to speak about; it is put to the would-be priests alone but it concerns you all. "Will you give your faithful diligence always so to minister the doctrine and sacraments and the discipline of Christ, as the Lord hath commanded . . . so that you may teach the people to keep and observe the same?"

Doctrine, sacraments, discipline: these are going to be your concern. The phrase might have been the doctrine of the Christian faith, or the sacraments of the gospel, or the discipline of the Church. We might have expected any of those phrases. But no: the question is so framed as to bring you right into the presence of the Lord Jesus. Christ's doctrine, Christ's sacraments, Christ's discipline are entrusted to you; and all "as the Lord hath commanded"—his command will be your motive and your clue.

1. *The doctrine of Christ.* That will be your theme. We don't preach or teach nearly enough about Christ himself. It is Christ whom the people need to hear about and to know. I sometimes put this question to myself: "Looking back to all the sermons I have preached in the past, say, six months, what have they told the people about Christ or done to make Christ visible to them? Do they know more about Christ at the end of them?" Ask yourself this question sometimes. Again, there are times when you feel helpless about what to preach, what text, what theme, and you are very blank and very stale. Say to yourself "What can I tell them about our Lord—some little part of the picture of him?".

Now we have, it is true, the difficulties that modern study of the Gospels has brought. The methods of Form-Criticism have queried any idea that the Gospels give us a kind of photographic history and suggest that the history is indeed mixed up with the interpretation and preaching of the early Christian communities. I believe, however, that while we cannot claim for the Gospels the kind of historical character which the older commentators used to claim we are none the less given portraits of a figure whom the Church's preachers and evangelists could never have invented from their own imagination. There was a figure in history who made them to be what they were: they did not make him. And aided by their portraits we can know him not a little, and know him specially in that blending of "opposites" which the Gospels show us: authority and self-effacement, severity and

55

tenderness, loneliness and involvement in humanity, ceaseless energy and rest and calm in the midst of it: *semper agens, semper quietus*. And when you promise to minister the doctrine of Christ it will mean showing the people Christ himself. I am sure that the strange modern trend to combine an atheistic philosophy with a devotion to the Man Jesus is one more challenge to us to set the person of Jesus at the heart of our teaching about God. We hold together Jesus portrayed in the Gospels and Jesus as the living Lord in the midst of his people today: Jesus in the Bible, Jesus in the Blessed Sacrament.

But the doctrine of Christ means far more than the historic Jesus. We are pledged to preach "the faith", the doctrines of Christianity in their bearing upon the lives of men and women and children. We have given to us the pattern of belief set out in the Creed, from "God the Father Almighty" right through to "the resurrection of the body and the life of the world to come". Do not treat the doctrines of the Creed as a string of impersonal items, like a row of bricks picked out of a box. Treat them as doctrines of Christ, as so many aspects of the mystery of which he is the centre. Thus the Father Almighty declares his almighty power most chiefly in showing mercy and pity—in the mercy and pity of Christ's Incarnation. Again, the Holy Catholic Church is Christ's family, Christ's household. The Communion of Saints is the company of those who reflect Christ's glory, and heaven is the enjoyment of Christ's radiance. See Christian doctrine in this way, and it will make all the difference to your study of it. Study gets very irksome if you think of it as adding more and more items of knowledge to your bag. Think of study rather as being refreshed from the deep, sparkling well of truth which is Christ himself. Study in this way does not stuff our already over-stuffed minds. Rather does it refresh us with new understanding and wonder. I love the phrase in the Ember collect "replenish them with the truth of thy doctrine".

2. You will promise to minister the *Sacraments of Christ*. Their meaning to you as you celebrate them, and their meaning to those whom you teach about them, will turn upon the freshness of your faith in Christ whose sacraments they are. In the Series II Confirmation Service the candidates are asked "Do you turn to Christ?" How real that question and answer can be depends upon the Church's ability to show that all the sacraments are Christ's act, the touch of the hand of Christ upon human lives through visible media. Teach them not only the Real Presence in the Eucharist but about Christ whose presence it is. Your own ministrations will need again and again to be made alive by your own realization of Christ.

3. You will promise to minister the *discipline of Christ*. How are we to understand that? No doubt the authors of the Ordinal had in mind the ecclesiastical discipline in the technical sense, the rules of behaviour which the Church enjoins upon its members. In the total context of scripture and history we can see the discipline of Christ as including all the duty and privilege of the common life of the Church as Christ's family. The Church's feasts are the great family days of the household. Almsgiving is our service to Christ in the needs of his household and as often as possible in the needs of suffering humanity, where to serve those who suffer is to serve Christ himself. So too the discipline of Christ will include the moral life of the Christian as he sets himself to follow Christ's way, accept Christ's yoke, and learn Christ's freedom. Christian morality includes God's laws, for God has been good enough to give humanity laws for the ordering of its life: the primacy of love and the rule of the Holy

Spirit do not remove law from its due place within Christian ethics. But all is part of the discipline of Christ, and people will not take it from us on the basis of a peremptory authority. They will take it as they are drawn to love Christ and to know Christ's love for them. That is how we bring the discipline of Christ to them.

So be ready for the question "Will you give your faithful diligence to minister the doctrine and the sacraments and the discipline of Christ as the Lord hath commanded?" Through the coming years you will be ministering doctrine and sacraments and discipline. It will become your profession, your stock-in-trade, and there will come monotony, professionalism, habit, staleness, tiredness, perfunctoriness. And just because you will be doing it ceaselessly the hard thing will be to keep alive the realization of Christ, the lively faith in Christ to whom it all belongs. That is the great issue by which you will be judged, both as life goes on and at the final day. Let me tell you, from experience of forty years as a priest, of three things which help.

1. First, try to recapture the sense of wonder. Pray to be renewed in the sense of wonder, quietly realizing what a wonderful thing it is to celebrate the Eucharist, what a wonderful thing it is that you are set where you are set as Christ's deacon or priest: deeper still, the wonder of your creation in God's own image, for that is the real ground of all wonder. "I thank thee O God for I am fearfully and wonderfully made".

2. Next, let the griefs, pains, humiliations which come to you help you. You will hate them, as they always hurt. But they help you to be near to Christ, and you will be learning not to fear them. There is the pain of disappointment when some

58

cherished plan has gone wrong, and you are inclined to be bitter and resentful—but let it help you to think more about Christ's pain and disappointment, and you are nearer to him and it becomes very different. There is the pain sometimes of the opposition, or misunderstanding, or abuse perhaps, coming to you from other people: it can feel terrible, but again—near to Christ. What if it is a part of the discipline of Christ which we profess to believe in? There is the pain which comes from one's own past mistakes coming home to roost. But that can bring one back to the truth of one's own inadequacies and the greatness of Christ's forgiveness, to the decrease of self and the increase of him. These things are not things which we do or seek; they just come. They will come to you. When they come let them help you to be a little nearer Christ crucified; that is how we find the deep joy of priesthood. You will know how truly the Psalmist says "Thou of very faithfulness hast caused me to be troubled".

3. Third, there is what we learn from the people around us about Christ, and the truths of our faith. You will be teaching about the Cross and the Resurrection and the love of God and the call to saintliness. And when you tend to become stale and perfunctory and unreal you will find yourself taught and enlivened by the people you work amongst. You talk year after year about the patience of the Cross: you will be finding it in a man or a woman who shows you what it means and *you* will be revived. You teach year after year about joy, and when you yet get stale and worse you will see Christian joy and *you* will be revived. For all the apathy and secularism and moral corruption around us, these Christians bring to life the faith entrusted to us.

I mention these helps which experience will bring; be ready

for them; and you will know more and more, and other people will know more and more, that the doctrine and the sacraments and the discipline belong to Christ, because you belong to Christ yourself.

Tomorrow it will happen: the great day for you and for Christ whose day it will be. You can now do no more to make ready. In the little time left of this Retreat, and again tonight, thank God with all your heart for his great goodness, for the joy which is Christ's and the joy which is going to be yours.

9

THE ORDINATION GOSPEL

Let your loins be girded and your lamps burning, and be like men who are waiting for their master to come home from the marriage feast, so that they may open to him at once when he comes and knocks. Blessed are those servants whom the master finds awake when he comes; truly, I say to you, he will gird himself and have them sit at table, and he will come and serve them. If he comes in the second watch, or in the third, and finds them so, blessed are those servants.

But know this, that if the householder had known at what hour the thief was coming, he would have been awake and would not have left his house to be broken into. You also must be ready; for the Son of Man is coming at an hour you do not expect.

Peter said: "Lord, are you telling the parable for us or for all?" And the Lord said: "Who then is the faithful and wise steward whom his master will set over his household, to give them their portion of food at the proper time? Blessed is the servant whom his master when he comes will find so doing. Truly I tell you he will set him over all his possessions. But if that servant says to himself 'my master is delayed in coming',

and begins to beat the menservants and the maidservants and to eat and drink and get drunk, the master of that servant will come on a day when he does not expect him and at an hour he does not know, and will punish him and put him with the unfaithful".
(Luke 12.35–46)

I intend to speak to you about the Gospel which will be read at the Ordination tomorrow. But I include a further section of the passage from St Luke beyond the portion which is read in the service. You notice that there is a string of parables and images following one another in quick succession:

1. Servants are waiting for their master's return from a wedding.
2. He returns, and instead of bidding them get his supper and wait on him he waits on them himself.
3. The picture changes. Watch, in case a burglar breaks in at an unexpected hour.
4. The true steward keeps things in order and is responsible to his lord. The bad steward misuses his authority by self-indulgence and by bullying.

We follow the series of rapidly changing pictures.

I

We are servants, called upon to obey. Has not the idea of obedience as a Christian virtue rather slipped out of our contemporary religion? We think much about the responses of faith, love, sonship, friendship in our relation to God or to our Lord. But obedience? We tend to think that it smacks of legalism, and not to dwell upon it. But it has an ineradicable place in the New Testament. Jesus was "obedient unto death" (Phil. 2.8), and "he learned obedience through what he suffered" (Heb. 5.8). The apostle is Christ's slave. It follows that besides our responses with the motive of faith or love there are also our responses with the motive of obeying God in doing this or that because we believe it to be his will. "If you love me you will keep my commandments" (John 14.15).

Our obedience calls for "loins girded" and "lamps burning".

"Loins girded" suggests an alertness which is ready to meet emergencies and interruptions. Do not be encumbered. Be ready to move, rapidly and unexpectedly. Our faithfulness is again and again tested by our power to deal with interruptions. You plan your day according to some rule, with so many hours for this and so many for that. Then all seems thrown into disorder by interruptions. You fail to do all that you set out to do, and you may get hot and bothered, and feel that what you planned as order has turned to chaos. But think of it in terms of the will of God. If the will of God is that you should accept this or that interruption, and you accept them with gladness, then a day which might seem tempestuous is really filled with plan and peace and order; for where the will of God is there is God's presence and God's peace, and where that will is obeyed there is pattern and harmony. In his will is your peace.

"Lamps burning". Here, it has been said, is the lesson of the Parable of the Ten Virgins compressed into two words. You will be ready not only to welcome a coming of the Lord but to go out to meet him.

So with loins girded and lamps burning we are ready to be good servants who obey the will of our Lord, both in what we know already to be his will and in what may at any moment be seen to be his will. I have often been helped by a prayer which is included in the old edition of the *Priest's*

Book of Private Devotion (it is attributed to a not very inspiring person, Pope Clement VI):

> Volo quidquid vis,
> Volo quia vis,
> Volo quomodo vis,
> Volo quamdiu vis.

I commend to you the "four Q's". They often help me when duties are irksome and one is saying, "Do I really have to do this?" or "I cannot stick this for much longer". *Quidquid*, if God wills it, God's presence will be in it, however tiresome it may be. *Quia*, if God wills it, this becomes the motive. *Quomodo*, we are to do it not just in the way we might ourselves have planned, for the *how* is in God's hands. *Quamdiu*, I must be ready to do this for as long as God wills that I should.

II

Watch and be ready for the Lord's coming. This is the theme both of the parable of the servants waiting to open the door when the master returns (verses 35–6) and of the parable of the burglar coming at an unadvertised hour (verses 39–40).

Think of your ministry as a series of comings of Christ, and the more you learn not to be taken unawares the more you can "love his appearing". How does he come? In times of your grief and disappointment he comes; and just when you begin to be oppressed you find that your nearness to *his* grief is the supreme fact: you are near his Cross again, and you are taken out of yourself. In times of joy in your ministry he comes; and just when you are tempted to be pleased with your own success you find that *his* joy is the supreme fact, and it makes an enormous difference. And in times of your complacency or unfaithfulness he comes; and in your sudden painful awareness that it is not well with you he is near in judgement and forgiveness. Watch and be ready. It happens as unexpectedly as the burglar breaking in.

But when the master of the house comes, what does he do? We would expect him to sit down and refresh himself, and tell the servants to wait on him. But no. The Lord waits on them. So the Lord always comes to us in order to serve us; and it is for us to let him. Occupied as we are in our ministry with serving him and serving the people in his name, we have to face the sharpest test of our humility, which is our readiness to let him serve us. He never comes to us without the longing to serve us. "Jesus, who served the apostles in washing their feet: serve me often, serve me daily, in washing my motives, my ambitions, my actions." "Cleanse me from my secret faults."

III

Peter now intervenes. "Lord, are you telling this parable for us, or for all?" I love to think that this is one of the touches of ironic humour which occur in St Luke's Gospel: "Is this for us apostles, or for everybody?", or in our modern speech: "Is this a parable for everyone, or is it specially for the clergy?"

It is for the apostles—it is for those whom Christ designates as stewards with authority in his household—for his answer to Peter's question is at once to describe the steward in the household as the man entrusted with immense, delegated authority. But, the parable continues, the steward in authority must not lord it over his subordinates, beating the menservants and maidservants; and he must not use the opportunities of his authority for self-indulgence, drinking and becoming drunk. Yes, Peter: the parable is for the apostles; it concerns their authority and the humility with which it must be exercised.

Tomorrow you will receive authority. Make no mistake, the authority is real and tremendous. The bishop who ordains you has authority in Christ's name to be the minister through those prayer and action Christ's authority is given to you in his Church.

> Take thou authority to execute the office of a deacon in the Church of God. . . .
> Receive the Holy Ghost for the office and work of a priest in the Church of God. . . .
> Take thou authority to preach the word of God and to minister the holy sacraments. . . .

I recall the classic words of Richard Hooker concerning this authority. I wonder if you know them?

> Is not God alone the Father of spirits? Are not souls the purchase of Jesus Christ? What angel in heaven could have said to man, as our Lord said to Peter, "Feed my sheep: preach, baptize; do this in remembrance of me; whose sins ye retain they are retained, and their offences pardoned whose faults you shall on earth forgive?" What think ye? Are these terrestrial sounds, or else are they voices uttered out of the clouds above? The power of the Ministry of God translateth out of darkness into glory; it raiseth men from the earth, and bringeth God himself down from heaven; by blessing visible elements it maketh them invisible grace; it givest daily the Holy Ghost, it hath to dispose of the flesh which was given for the life of the world, and that blood which was poured out to redeem souls; when it poureth malediction upon the heads of the wicked they perish; when it revoketh the

same they revive. O wretched blindness, if we admire not so great power, more wretched if we consider it aright and notwithstanding imagine that any but God could bestow it.[1]

In such words one of our greatest Anglican divines describes the authority of the steward in the Lord's household.

By your humility you will prove that the authority entrusted to you is really Christ's. The warnings of the parable still stand. You are not likely to start beating the menservants and the maidservants: but everyone possessing authority is liable to become bossy and overbearing. "It shall not be so with you." You are not likely to drink too much and become drunk (though some do have this trouble, and in the Pastoral Epistles the deacons are warned not to be addicted to too much wine), but every one possessing privilege and security is liable to a subtle worldly enjoyment. Again "it shall not be so with you". But if it is not to be so with you, you will again and again recapture the earlier parable about Christ being *your* servant. Let him serve you in the frequent cleansing of motive, ambition, and action; and then your authority, possessed in his name. will be wielded always with the humility which is his.

I leave you with these thoughts about the Gospel to which we shall be listening tomorrow and the parables which follow it. Go back to it sometimes in later years. It will help you year by year to be ready for the comings of Christ.

[1] *Laws of Ecclesiastical Polity V*, 77.1

10

ST PETER'S CHARGE

"So I exhort the elders among you as a fellow elder and a witness of the sufferings of Christ as well as a partaker in the glory that is to be revealed. Tend the flock of God that is your charge, not by constraint but willingly; not for shameful gain but eagerly, not as domineering over those in your charge but being examples to the flock. And when the chief shepherd is manifested you will obtain the unfading crown of glory.

Likewise you that are younger be subject to the elders. Clothe yourselves, all of you, with humility towards one another, for God opposes the proud but gives grace to the humble.

Humble yourselves therefore under the mighty hand of God, that in due time he may exalt you. Cast all your anxieties on him, for he cares about you. Be sober, be watchful. Your adversary the devil prowls around like a roaring lion, seeking someone to devour. Resist him, firm in your faith, knowing that the same experience of suffering is required of your brotherhood throughout the world. And after you have suffered a little while, the God of all grace, who has called you to his eternal glory in Christ, will himself

restore, establish and strengthen you. To him be the domin-ion for ever and ever. Amen."
(1 Peter 5.1–11)

St Peter is addressing the presbyters and charging them about the various relationships in which they stand—to Christ, to one another within the ministry, to the people whom they serve, and to the world around them. If I now ask you to dwell specially upon St Peter's counsels on our relation with one another within the ordained ministry you will see at once that this relation is inseparable from the larger context of the other relations.

How vividly does the history of St Peter seem to come to life in what he writes. *Gird yourselves with humility* recalls the feet-washing at the last supper. *A partaker in the glory that is to be revealed* may recall the Transfiguration when three disciples had a fore-glimpse of the future glory. *Tend the flock* recalls the words of Jesus to Peter by the Lake of Galilee after the Resurrection. *I exhort the elders among you as a fellow elder*: St Peter addresses the presbyters as one who speaks with apostolic authority and is also their fellow presbyter. So today the bishop who ordains you to be priests will always be your fellow presbyter: nothing means more to him than to be still, with you, a priest in the Church of God.

Tend the flock of God that is in your charge. Here is a sentence to meditate upon again and again. Your tending of the flock is to have three characteristics. *Not of constraint but willingly*. Here the contrast is between the service which runs on with the mechanical force of habit or tradition—just "carrying on"—and the service which is based upon a succession of deliberate acts of the will. Day by day you consider how there is a will of Christ that this and that should be done; day by day you deliberately embrace this will in setting about your tasks—"I come to do thy will, O my God". Catch the meaning of the word ἑκουσίως, and it can make all the difference to the spirit of your work. Then, *not for shameful gain but eagerly*. There is little chance of "shameful gain" for you in a material sense. But something akin to it, and equally irrelevant to our calling, can worry us: a concern about "status". Such a concern is irrelevant, because for all of us the one status that matters is the status of proximity to Jesus, who says to us "where I am, there shall my servant be also" (John 12.26), on Calvary or wherever he may will. And the alternative to "for shameful gain" is "eagerly", προθύμως. It is as you press on after Jesus in eager enthusiasm that you forget the irrelevancies of status. *Not as domineering . . . but as being examples*. You will not lord it over the people, hector them, drive them, or boss them. You will lead them in the right direction by your example, not least by your example of humility towards God and your fellows, for that is the way they, like you, will need to go. So think sometimes of these three pairs of opposites which St Peter gives us as the way in which we tend the flock. Nothing may help you in this more than the next words: *when the chief shepherd is manifested you will obtain the never fading crown of glory*. Heaven is the goal, the goal of priesthood, the goal of every member of the flock, the goal of man created in God's image to share eternally in God's glory. Think far more often about heaven, for *there* is the true perspective for our ministry from day to day.

Then comes the sentences about mutual relations within the ministry. *You that are younger be subject to the elders*. It is uncertain whether this refers to office or to seniority in years, and it would be wrong to exclude either reference. You promise at the ordination to "reverently obey your Ordinary and other chief Ministers unto whom is committed the charge and government over you; following with a glad mind and will their godly admonitions, and submitting yourselves to their godly judgements". But this important deference of younger to older is in the context of the humility of all towards all. *Clothe yourselves, all of you, with humility towards one another.* All of us are to treat one another with humility. The Archbishop whom you promise to obey reverently is himself called to be humble towards you, learning from you as well as teaching you, as we all try to learn Christ through our dealings with one another. It is about this, in our contemporary scene, that I would say a little more.

Our relations with one another in the priesthood are an important part of our service of Christ and the people. When the clergy, older and younger, serve one another and learn from one another the whole Church is healthier. But it is easy for these relations to go wrong.

Some of the faults lend themselves to jest and caricature. There is *vicaritis*: the vicar who is absurdly status-conscious in relation to his colleagues and does not see that by learning something of the mind of the new curate he will be able to teach him more and also gain in understanding of his own younger parishioners. But there is also *curatitis*: the curate can be cocksure about his own recently acquired notions and not be aware that they are not as new as he thinks they are, and that even if they are true they need to be relearnt in the rough and tumble of pastoral work before their validity is assured. But if those faults belong to the particular relation of vicar and curate, there are also faults which belong to the entire range of clerical relationships. One of these is jealousy. It is a poison which spreads more easily than you would think. You can be jealous of a man because he has gifts which you would like. You can be jealous of a man because while you think he lacks your gifts he seems to be more successful than you. You can be jealous of a man because some of the people look to him when you thought of them as *your* people looking to you for spiritual help. In this case your love for people, through its intensity of feeling, can make you jealous, as you think of them as *your* spiritual children. Thus complex are the elements which create pastoral jealousy; when we have disentangled the elements we can see what the remedies may be. I leave this exercise for you to work out.

There is also partisanship which can be wrecking to the right relation between priests. Let those who are glad to be Catholics or Evangelicals or Liberals set themselves to learn all they can from one another, for the partisan can soon become a person who loves his own apprehension of the truth more than Christ who is the truth, and himself more than either. If today there is less conscious partisanship around the old labels than there used to be, there can be the more subtle partisanship of facile contentment with one's own set of assumptions and attitudes which can be no less partial for being unlabelled in the formal sense. What am I learning from my neighbours, contemporary or older or younger?

But perhaps the greatest strains in fellowship may be between the generations. There is nothing new in this kind of tension. When I was ordained in the nineteen-twenties we used to be conscious of the difference between ourselves and those ordained near the beginning of the century with the chasm of the 1914–1918 war between us and them. Perhaps at the present time the tension of the generations is greater than usual as the changes in society in the last few years have been cataclysmic in speed and character, and a particular feature of the young today is the rejection of tradition and the appeal to history. The "sense of the past" means little to those who live, think, and feel within the frontiers of the "present".

Let me make a few suggestions about these tensions. (a) Pierce down deep in theology, spirituality, religious language, pastoral method, and you discover what is neither modern and contemporary or old and archaic but genuinely *timeless*. Then you find both in theological reading and in comradeship with other priests the distinction between what belongs to this or that time and what belongs to all time or to no time. It is an exciting discovery. (b) Remember that some of us older men were once the progressives or even the radicals, and now we are outmoded. If you are one of today's progressives or radicals you will be outmoded soon. The true *radical* is not the man who suspends himself from the branches on either the left or the right, but the man who in his thinking and action goes to the *root* of the tree.

In these ways the younger and the older learn from one another. Maintain your integrity, your power of criticism: be yourself. And at the same time let humility, forbearance, and a love of people both young and old help you to enjoy and to strengthen fellowship across the decades.

After charging the older and the younger to have humility towards one another, St Peter continues: *Humble yourselves therefore under the mighty hand of God, that in due time he may exalt you. Cast all your anxieties on him, for he cares about you.* It is the thought of God's majestic sovereignty and providential care of you which keeps you humble. Notice the cumulative force in the words about humility which early Christians could use. There is ταπεινότης, the state of lowliness, the word known in the pagan world. There is the newly created Christian word ταπεινοφροσύνη, lowliness of *mind*; and you remember St Paul's words "have this mind among yourselves which you have in Christ Jesus" (Phil. 2.5). And in the present passage there is a kind of violence about the middle or passive verb ταπεινωθήτε, "be humiliated". It is by humiliations, such

73

as St Peter's readers were expecting in Asia Minor, that humility is learnt. We must not fear humiliations: we are under God's sovereign hand and loving care. Well is this, for your adversary the devil *prowls around like a roaring lion, seeking someone to devour*. The peril to St Peter's presbyters may have been apostasy when persecution fell upon them. The peril to you is more likely to be the apostasy of a kind of subtle secularization of religion and ministry, the supernatural elements losing their hold upon you. Therefore you must *watch and pray*, knowing that you do this not alone but as sharing in the Gethsemane ministry of Jesus. *Resist him firm in your faith*. The definite article is used, and we might translate either "your faith" or "the faith". The one is the depth of your own personal commitment to Jesus, which makes you proof against the enemy. The other is the massive testimony of the faith of the Church handed down through the centuries, the faith which is your home and your country. Both aspects of faith are yours, and given by God. Then come the words of immense comfort, *knowing that the same experience of suffering is required of your brotherhood throughout the world*. When you have your own "sufferings" remember your fellow Christians in parts of the world where Christian faithfulness means an endurance and fortitude beyond any experience of our own. It is well for us often to bear such fellow Christians in our minds, and the recollection of our "brotherhood throughout the world" gives the true perspective for our own little troubles.

So the charge of St Peter moves to its climax. He bids us set the present interlude of our service and our frustration beside the *eternal glory in Christ*. We ought to think much and often about heaven. See how the hope of heaven enters the thought of this Epistle again and again. Heaven is, after all, the proper destiny of man who is created in God's own image. It is the goal towards which we are leading the people whom our Lord has entrusted to us. Nor is it so far away, as it is anticipated in the present life in Christ, and not least in eucharistic worship. He who called you to become a priest or a deacon tomorrow has also called you to *eternal glory in Christ*, and there will lie the true perspective of diaconate and priesthood.

I recall to you St Peter's charge. Let it prepare you for tomorrow. And read it from time to time in the future years. It will help you not only to look forward to the *eternal glory in Christ* but to find it in the midst of your present labours.

11

DIVINE HUMILITY

Everyone who exalts himself will be abased,
and he who humbles himself will be exalted.

(Luke 18.14)

In these words our Lord sums up his parable of the complacent Pharisee and the penitent Publican. The contrast has
run on from the Jewish Church of our Lord's time into the
Christian Church in every period; and it recurs today in
every parish and in every congregation. You will find in
your ministry what a drag the one kind of character is upon
the life of the Church and what a source of strength is the
other. Indeed to lead men and women from the one state to
the other will be one of the chief aims of your pastoral work.

The words, however, which occur in a number of contexts
in the Gospel tradition, have far wider reference. They
concern the predicament of the human race and the answer
of the Gospel to that predicament. Here is Man satisfied
with himself and with his immense powers and using his
powers to aggrandize himself in ways which make the world
divided and miserable. And here on the other side is the

answer of the gospel, that if Man has lost the power to humble himself before his Creator the Creator will humble himself towards his creatures. So the divine humility breaks upon the scene of human pride. Bethlehem, Calvary, the feet-washing at the Last Supper, all say "he who humbles himself will be exalted". The saying of Jesus is echoed in the hymn which St Paul cites in Philippians 2, telling of how one who was in the form of God humbled himself and God highly exalted him. Divine humility is the power which comes to make the human race different. I recall some words of St Augustine: "So low had human pride sunk us that only divine humility could raise us up" (*Sermons*, 118). Of this gospel and this power you will, a few hours hence, become the deacon or the priest.

All Christians are called to be humble. But the ordained man sets forward the gospel and the sacraments whereby their humility is sustained, and leads them in the way of humility as their pastor. He acts with Christ's commission and Christ's authority, and what can humble him more than to be the steward of the mysteries of the God who humbled himself? Recall how some of the descriptions of the apostolic ministry in the New Testament bring this out:

> Truly, truly I say to you, a servant is not greater than his Lord: nor he who is sent greater than he who sent him. (John 13.10)

> What we preach is not ourselves, but Jesus Christ as Lord, with ourselves your servants for Jesus' sake. (2 Cor. 4.3)

> We have this treasure in earthen vessels to show that the transcendent power belongs to God and not to us. (2 Cor. 4.7)

> Clothe yourselves, all of you, with humility towards one another. (1 Peter 5.5)

77

Your humility therefore will be the condition of a ministry which represents our Lord and makes him known and loved, and enables people to have the awareness of God. We often lament that the very idea of God is so remote or so lacking. The word often seems to mean so little, and "if only", we say, "if only" the sense of God was present how different things would be. And how is the sense of God to be recovered? A host of considerations are relevant, and I am sure you have often discussed them: more reality in worship, more contemporary language, more intellectual integrity, more facing of the intellectual problems, more expression of theology in social action, more rediscoveries of truth, and the whole range of issue now under debate. Yet it remains that there is only one kind of *person* who makes God known and realized by other people, and that is the person who is humble because he knows God and knows God because he is humble. There is no substitute for this. It is only a humble priest who is authoritatively a man of God, one who makes God real to his fellows. May it one day be said of you, not necessarily that you talked about God cleverly, but that you made God real to people. "He somehow made God real to me": only humility can do that.

But how many are the snags! There will be everything in the world to thwart you. If you do well, you can be pleased with yourself, and humility is in peril. If you do badly, you may worry about yourself, and humility is in peril. If people are nice to you and tell you what a good clergyman you are, humility is in peril. If people are nasty to you, you have a grievance, and humility is in peril. Furthermore, the temptations to jealousy between us in the ministry are more subtle and common than you may realize.[1] So too, if you are learning to be humble, you are in peril. You can half-

[1] See also p. 71.

consciously congratulate yourself that you are a spiritually minded priest unlike the worldly, pompous, ill-trained, Erastian clergyman in the next parish. We all know some of the caricatures of the man who, knowing he is meant to be humble, affects it in pious mannerisms of speech and habit.

What of ambition? If we have the supreme ambitions of serving Christ's kingdom, of bringing people to Christ, of becoming ourselves like Christ in the power of his Resurrection and the fellowship of his sufferings (see St Paul's description of this ambition in Philippians 3.10–14), then unworthy ambitions lose their grip. Yet such is Christ's tenderness towards our natural propensities that we need not rule out specific ambitions of doing certain things "well" and fulfilling our particular office "well". Is not the heart to be warmed from time to time by the "well done, good and faithful servant" applied to this or that task or office? And as there is a kind of ambition which is lawful and right, so there is a kind of smug disclaiming of ambition which is as spiritually poisonous as it is unattractive. The sound rule is that all our ideas of doing well, of winning praise, and of ambitions in achievement should be within the supreme motive of the humility of Christ. The man who is truly humble can use and accept ambitions and praises because his soul is filled with the glorifying of God. So with authority. There are times when in using your authority you must, in a sense, assert yourself: avoid the false meekness of timidity. But assert yourself with that authority which humbles you because it is not your own but Christ's.

Here are a few counsels for the struggle which will be before you.

Thank God, often and always. Just now you are full of thankfulness for God's great goodness to you. But there will come through the years a tendency to take God's goodness for granted. Thank God, carefully and wonderingly, for your continuing privileges and for every experience of his goodness. Thankfulness is a soil in which pride does not easily grow.

Take care about *confession of your sins*. As time passes the habit of being critical about people and things grows more than each of us may realize. So be sure to criticize yourself in God's presence: that is your self-examination. And put yourself under the divine criticism: that is your confession. Then God's forgiveness renews your freedom to be humble. If you do use sacramental confession, do not slip out of using it. If you do not use sacramental confession, ask yourself if it would not be a good thing that you should.

Be ready to accept *humiliations*. They can hurt terribly, but they help you to be humble. There can be the trivial humiliations. Accept them. There can be the bigger humiliations: some cherished plan misfires, or some injustice is done to you, or some slight and affront, or some sorrow, or some trouble caused by a mistake of your own. All these can be so many chances to be a little nearer to our humble and crucified Lord. There is nothing to fear if you are near to our Lord and in his hands.

Do not worry about *status*. One reason why I grieve that, so far, the *Partners in Ministry* proposals have not been accepted is that they would do a good deal to break down status divisions amongst us clergymen: we should have the same pay in accordance with years of service, and "titular" distinctions would be on the way out. Be that as it may, there is only one status that our Lord bids us be concerned with, and that is the status of proximity to himself. "If a man serve me, let him follow me, and where I am, there also shall my servant be." (John 12.26) That is our status: to be near to our Lord wherever he may ask us to go with him.

Use your *sense of humour*. Laugh about things, laugh at the absurdities of life, laugh about yourself, and about your own absurdity. We are all of us infinitesimally small and ludicrous creatures within God's universe. You have to be serious, but never be solemn, because if you are solemn about anything there is the risk of becoming solemn about yourself.

I give you these few counsels about the ways of keeping faithful to the divine humility which is the secret of Christ's commission to you tomorrow and of your execution of it through the coming years. Through the years people will thank God for you. And let the reason for their thankfulness be not just that you were a person whom they liked or loved but because you made God real to them. "He made God real to us." It is God's design for you, that people should say that about you. Is is possible? Is it credible? Do not speculate. Do not worry. Put yourself in God's hands in joy and thankfulness. And let St Peter have the last word, in his own charge to the presbyters: "Humble yourselves under the mighty hand of God, that he may exalt you in due time, casting all your cares upon him, for he cares for you." (1 Peter 5.6–7)

12

FRET NOT THYSELF
BECAUSE OF THE UNGODLY

Fret not thyself because of the ungodly.

(Psalm 37.1)

Is this rather a negative charge to give you on the eve of your ordination: "Don't fret"? No, the Christian gospel is largely concerned with the issue of fretting and not fretting. We live in a fretting world, and the gospel can be paraphrased "fret not, only believe". More particularly, the people to whom you minister will be full of frettings, and you will be leading them from fretting into Christian peace. But as you do this the spirit of fretting will press persistently against your own defences. You may fret through your Christian sympathy with people's griefs. You may fret about troubles and frustrations in the Church, where there is a good deal of "loss of nerve". You may fret about your own failures and disappointments. And your own fretting may weaken your witness to the joy of the gospel. Therefore it is right for me to charge you "fret not".

There is certainly much to fret about. In the world there are ugly and frightening spectres: the contrasts of affluence and poverty; racial conflict mounting higher; the drift of the Western democracies into spiritual aimlessness. Who would not fret with these spectres at the door? Not only the world but the Church as an institution makes you fret. Many, I know, find it difficult to serve it with happy contentment. Sometimes it frets by its old-fashionedness, its inability to reform itself, its shirking of challenging issues. And sometimes it frets in the opposite way: by a seeming loss of historic values, by a playing down of the supernatural, by a concern to be "with it". If we are ourselves conceited, we fret about what others in the Church are doing or not doing in a "we and they" superiority; if we are humble, we include ourselves within the criticism. In either case, we may fret; and a kind of nervous fretting can bedevil the Church's life. So the world may fret you, the Church may fret you, and there will be the frettings of a more personal kind always round the corner. Tiredness, monotony, staleness, the small results which seem to come from immense expenditure of labour. So, all in all, there will be times when you find yourself saying, "Who will show us any good?"

So a mist comes to hide from your awareness some of the realities in which you believe: sin and judgement, mercy and joy. The answer is drawn from the scriptures, from our divine Lord, from the lives of the saints, and from your own experience as a Christian. The answer is a deep, sparkling well of truth, which is Christ himself, and from it our fears are washed away and our thirsty spirits are refreshed.

First, when you fret about the world and wonder whether God has gone away or whether God is "dead", turn to the doctrine of *Judgement*. Recapture the lost biblical theme of judgement. God is indeed here—but here in judgement upon a world which has wandered from his righteousness. Let the prophets and the apostles speak to us again of how nations which neglect God, stifle conscience, and prefer selfishness do bring calamity upon themselves. That is what is happening in our world. God has not disappeared: God is here—in judgement. As the Psalmist vividly puts it, "he gave them their hearts' desire, and sent leanness withal into their souls". Turn your fretting into the thought that God is here as Judge—and you will once again be near to God himself. Knowing God's nearness as judge, we know at once his nearness also in mercy and forgiveness.

So the God whom we accept as here in judgement is at once known to us as here in sovereignty, the sovereignty of a faithful creator. The world is in his hands. But, the gospel teaches us, it is a sovereignty which is only and always the sovereignty of self-giving love, of Cross and Resurrection, of life through death; the sovereignty of suffering transfigured. There our fretting has its supreme answer. You know this already in your theological study, for you have read great books about the union of love and omnipotence, of the Lamb and the Throne. You know it a little already in your own experience. But you will in your ministry be learning from some of the people you deal with how suffering can, through the nearness of Christ, be made wonderfully different. You will see the truth of Cross and Resurrection in men and women whom you try to serve.

Then there is our fretting about the Church. One word only. Remember that the Church is both divine and human. It is *human*, inasmuch as its members all share in our sinful and fallible human nature. Thus our "we and they" talk about the Church melts into our contrition. It is *divine*, inasmuch as the principle of its life is the risen Jesus and the Holy Spirit, whose presence the sins of Christians never prevent being somewhere at work. Let us then be as critical, as discontented as we may be, and never complacent. But our discontent, without losing its integrity or its sharpness, will not turn into fretting if we remember that it is God who judges and Church in its human element, and after judging can raise up a faithful remnant.

Whenever fretting threatens to get you down, turn to our Lord. He is grieving. Think of *his sorrow*, and the sting of self-pity will be drawn from yours. We should often recall the scene when our Lord drew near to the city of Jerusalem and wept over it saying, "If you had known the things that belong to your peace, but now they are hid from your eyes". Every ordained man must come near to this grief of Jesus, seeing with his eyes, feeling with his heart. We learn that any disappointment, any setback, any personal sorrow, or any wound to our pride can be made different if we are near to the grief of Jesus. You will have the experience of being able, after some grievous happening, to say, "It is good for me that I have been in trouble". May you have the faith in Christ that can go a step further and say, with another of the Psalms, "Thou of every faithfulness hast caused me to be troubled".

Then there is our thanksgiving and our penitence. We are taught in our years of training that thanksgiving is the heart of prayer. It is, I know, in deep thanksgiving that you are approaching tomorrow's ordination. But as time passes, when the pressures of work mount up and the vexations multiply, it is all too easy, while giving thanksgiving its liturgical priority, to take it for granted—in other words to neglect it as a *personal* act. Be thankful to God. Take trouble in thinking over what you are thankful for, and in telling God of your thankfulness. Remember how the Greek word ἐξομολογοῦμαι is used both of "confessing" sins and "confessing" God's mercies. I believe that our neglect of the latter is an all too common failing.

So with your penitence. Nicholas Berdyaev wrote somewhere that one of the characteristics of Christianity is to transpose a sense of grievance into a sense of sin. It is the work of the gospel to bring about that transposition and so to expose human lives to the divine forgiveness. That will be your message, and your task with men and women and children. So nothing matters more than that this divine work should be repeating itself in you, turning the fretting of the natural man into the penitence of the man whose heart God has touched and renewing for you the miracle of forgiveness. We are poor priests if there is ever blurred in our consciousness either the recurring fact of divine forgiveness, or the wonder of its miraculous character. Here, surely, is the line between authentic Christianity and a secularized substitute for it.

So I give you these counsels about fretting, all of them drawn from the gospel and the wisdom of Christian experience. But the Psalm from which our text comes has itself wise counsel to give, prefiguring the Christian answer. Many times I have found that "the seventh evening of the month", when Psalm 37 is said, has revived my drooping courage.

Here are some of its counsels:

Be doing good. When depression comes, find at once something to do, and get on with it. Go and help someone.

Delight thou in the Lord. Let your heart go towards *him*.

Hold thee still in the Lord. Be quiet. Stop talking, to other people or to yourself. In stillness recover the true perspective.

Leave off from wrath. While you are bitter there can be no true perspective, no wise decision. Vision and judgement are clouded. And the secret is in the next quotation.

He shall make thy righteousness as clear as the light, and thy just dealing as the noonday. You do not have to vindicate yourself: God vindicates you as and when he knows best.

A small thing that the righteous hath is better than great riches of the ungodly. What is the small thing? Had you forgotten how precious it is, or had you "despised the day of small things"?

Dwell in the land and verily thou shalt be fed. Remember your inheritance, the Catholic Church of the ages, the country of the saints. Claim this as your own country and go on living in it.

I went by, and lo he was gone: I sought him, but his place could nowhere be found. If you are faithful you sometimes find that "tiresomeness" suddenly vanishes.

Tomorrow in the Ordination Service the answer of Jesus Christ to a fretting world will once again be proclaimed, and you will receive his commission and power to bring peace to many fretting lives. Many such lives will be healed and made strong by your teaching, your care and your love for them. At the Ordination there will be as in every sacrament the seen and the unseen part. You will see the Archbishop who ordains you and the many people who will be there praying for you. You will not see that which gives meaning to it all, and this is the re-enactment of what happened on the first Easter evening. Our Lord will be there, with the words "Peace be unto you, as the Father hath sent me, even so send I you"; and the words "Peace be unto you" go always with the wounds in his hands and his side. In the coming years you will know the wounds more than in the past, and you will also know the peace more than you know it now. And one day many will thank God for all that you will have done to make the wounds and the peace known to them.

13

SORROW AND JOY

As sorrowful, yet always rejoicing.
(2 Corinthians 6.10)

These words are part of St Paul's description of the life of an apostle, which ends with the majestic string of antitheses, "by honour and dishonour, by evil report and good report; as deceivers and yet true; as unknown and yet well known; as dying, and, behold, we live; as chastened, and not killed; as sorrowful, yet always rejoicing; as poor yet making many rich; as having nothing, and yet possessing all things". In part the description seems remote from our own likely experience as it tells of a life of persecution and physical hazards. But in part it tells of universal and permanent characteristics of Christian ministry, and nowhere is this more true than in the words which I have chosen for my charge for you, "as sorrowful yet always rejoicing". You are called by God to be a man who is sorrowful yet always rejoicing. This is bound up with the office to which you will be ordained tomorrow.

On the purely human level the words have an immediate

ring of truth. You are as a priest going to be exposed in new ways to joy and to sorrow.

Whenever I ask one of you after a year or two if you are enjoying it (perhaps it is a silly question), the answer is "yes", and I am sure the answer is sincere. You enjoy the many openings of touch with people of all kinds. You have range upon range of new human experiences: the small children, the teenagers, the young married people, the old. You get to know every kind of profession, and every kind of human circumstance. You are rewarded by many friendships. There are people who like you and say so; people who love you and say so. And with these joys for the natural man there are the joys of seeing closely the grace of God in human lives, in individuals and in families as they grow.

Yet it is also true that every ordained man sooner or later will be telling of his grief. The griefs, like the joys, occur on the purely human level. There is fatigue of body and mind. There can be worries about home and family. There is the monotony of times when the spark seems to go out and every day seems grey, damp, and foggy; and there comes the spiritual listlessness which the monks called *accidie*, a mood of lazy depression when we might be cynical or resentful if we had a little more energy in us. In contrast there is the grief that comes from spiritual alertness; you will sorrow at the apathy of thousands about the things of God, at your pastoral disappointments, at being let down by people on whom you had relied. There is grief at one's own blunders: "if only I hadn't put my foot in it like that". "As sorrowful"—the words come true for you.

So then both your joys and your griefs are going to be a mixture of many elements, physical and psychological, desirable and undesirable, godly and ungodly. There is the joy God wants to share with you, and the joy that is irrelevant or worse. There is the sorrow in Christ which is a gate to the knowledge of God, and the sorrow which injures and deadens. As St Paul says later in this same Epistle, "the sorrow of the world works death" (2 Cor. 7.10).

We see the extremes of contrast clearly enough in people we have known. Here is a priest, so cheerful, always cheerful, cheerful for the wrong reasons, cheerful in pride and shallowness; he may be liked and admired, but he will not become a true priest until his heart is broken, whether in penitence before his Lord or in agony for the people he is serving. And here is a priest always gloomy, always grumbling; and he tries to spiritualize his gloom into a kind of perpetual holy moan, so that he cannot even say the vestry prayer without a crack in his voice. I want to say to him, "For your penance read through the Epistle to the Philippians".

Now we turn to St Paul: "as sorrowful yet always rejoicing". He is describing in part the natural grief and the natural happiness of empirical experience in a temperament as sensitive as we know his to have been. But he is also describing how these human experiences and feelings are lifted up onto a supernatural plane, and on this supernatural plane there are two great truths to which the New Testament witnesses. (*a*) Joy and sorrow are joy and sorrow in the Lord. "Rejoice in the Lord" says St Paul to the Philippians. (*b*) Joy and sorrow are not things competing and conflicting: they are as sides of a single coin, like Cross and Resurrection.

Joy in the Lord. It is the joy experienced by those who, come what may, are beginning to know God, to enjoy God in his beauty and loveliness, and to be exposed to his energies. "The fruit of the Spirit is love, joy. . . ." (Gal. 5.22)

We find this joy in Old Testament writers, especially the Psalmists. "I will go unto the altar of God, the God of my joy and gladness." "My heart dances for joy." "Let Israel rejoice in him that made him." "My joy shall be in the Lord." What is this joy? It is not only the joy of a sure faith that God reigns supreme; it is the joy of a practical fellowship with one who is himself joy and pours joy into lives which are united with him. So the prophet Habakkuk finds that at a time when the fig tree is barren, and the vines bear no grapes, and the olive tree fails, and the orchards are empty, and the sheep and the cattle are gone he can say "yet I will rejoice in my God".

It is this practical companionship with God and exposure to his joy which the New Testament reaffirms with new vigour. At the root of the new experience is the divine forgiveness which flows from the Cross and the Resurrection of Jesus. In Romans 6. 1–11, we are shown how Christian joy flows from the new states of forgiveness, sonship and faith which Christ has brought. Our joy is the joy of those who are forgiven and forgiving. Lose hold on the realities of penitence and forgiveness in your life, and it will not be surprising if the joy which is your privilege begins to fade.

Nowhere is this joy seen more vividly than in the Epistle to the Philippians. Here the apostle records every characteristic incident of pastoral sadness. There is the squabble of two tiresome women, Euodia and Syntyche. There is the anxiety of the illness of his friend Epaphroditus. There is the wrecking influence of false teachers in the Church. There is the bad behaviour of some close to the apostle who preach Christ "in strife and envy". All this, before we mention that he is in prison and awaiting his trial. But because he can say "for me, to live is Christ" he says "rejoice in the Lord always". His readers, like himself, are exposed to the joy which flows from Christ to them.

To have joy in God means knowing that God is our country, our environment, the air we breathe. "God is the country of the soul", said St Augustine. Living in that country, we do not turn away from the griefs of our present environment—indeed we may expect a greater sensitivity to these—but we are in the perspective of God, of heaven, of eternity. I believe that much of the present obsession of our Church with doubts, uncertainties, negatives, loss of nerve, is due to a failure as a Church to live with God as the country of the soul. In that country we face problems with integrity, but we also share in the joy of the saints.

Now for the second truth. The joy and the sorrow are like two sides of a coin. The New English Bible translates the text "in our sorrow we always have a cause for joy". If this is a lapse from translating into paraphrasing, it certainly brings out a facet of the meaning.

Our Lord called the apostles to be with him, with him in the sorrow and the joy of his mission. He invited them to share in his baptism and his cup, and two of them confidently said "we are able". He told them at the Last Supper that they were those who had shared with him in his πειρασμοὶ. He invited three of them to share in his ministry of watching and praying in the Garden of Gethsemane, but sleep overcame them. In the event, Jesus was isolated and alone in his death: no one shared in it. But from the early days of the Church in the city of Jerusalem the new bond between the disciples and the suffering of Jesus had begun. "They rejoiced to be counted worthy to suffer for the name." To suffer with Christ became the hallmark of discipleship.

We are to share in Christ's sorrow, and the realm in which we do this is not the realm of a special kind of mystical experience, but the realm of everyday ministry. It does not mean that we are to be ashamed of our own little griefs or worries. We do not cease to be hurt and sensitive, and Christ understands our hurts and disappointments. But in and through them we are drawn near to Christ's sorrow. It makes all the difference. The setbacks, the plans that misfire, the unfairness of other people, the sickness, or whatever the trial may be—let these be the door into Christ's sorrow. And as he wept over the city of Jerusalem which did not know the things which belonged to its peace, so may he wish us to weep with him over the cities and villages and populations where his love is rejected or unknown and his people suffer. He draws us to watch with him, and to watch will mean to bear and to grieve.

But the door into his sorrow is also the door into his joy. As the cloud of the presence in the tabernacle was pierced from within by a burning light (νεφέλη φωτεινὴ), so the sorrow of Jesus is the place of reconciling love pouring itself into the world, and his joy there is radiant. "Ask and you shall receive that your joy may be full" (John 16.24): "Your joy no man takes from you" (John 16.22).

This is the joy that is deeper, more lasting, than the joys of our own satisfaction. Run a good parish, preach a good sermon, carry out a successful project, do a worthwhile piece of work; and you are pleased and happy. But this will not become the pleasure of pride and self-esteem if you are sharing in the joy of Jesus that his work is being done and people are being brought to him.

"As sorrowful yet always rejoicing." It is with this ahead of you that you will tomorrow become a deacon or a priest. It is for this that you are committing yourself to the Lord Jesus. "Lord, take my heart and break it: break it not in the way I would like, but in the way you know to be best. And, because it is you who break it, I will not be afraid, for in your hands all is safe and I am safe. Lord, take my heart and give to it your joy, not in the ways I like, but in the ways you know are best, that your joy may be fulfilled in me. So, dear Lord, I am ready to be your deacon, ready to be your priest."

14

THE BISHOP

It is a pity that there is a scarcity of books about the office and work of a bishop. Legions of books have been written about "episcopacy", but few or none about the inner life or the practical problems of a bishop at the present time. I wish one of my colleagues would do for his brethren and his successors what was done for bishops in an earlier age by Pope Gregory the Great in his *Regula Pastoralis*. This remarkable work[1] was written, as was St John Chrysostom's *On the Priesthood*, as a kind of apology for the author's shrinking from acceptance of the burden of the pastoral office. While its contents are related to priests in general as well as to bishops its emphasis upon pastoral *rule* made it especially a bishop's manual. It was as such that it won immense influence in many countries. Alcuin wrote to Eanbald, the Archbishop of York, in 796: "Wherever you go, let the pastoral book of St Gregory be your companion. Read and reread it often, that in it you may learn to know

[1] See St Gregory the Great, *Pastoral Care*, translated and annotated by Henry Davis S.J., Longmans, 1950.

yourself and your work, that you may have before your eyes how you ought to live and teach. The book is a mirror of the life of a bishop and a medicine for all the wounds inflicted by the devil's deception."[1] It was King Alfred the Great who, with the aid of some of his clergy, translated the work into West Saxon, wishing that every bishop in England should be given a copy. In the Carolingian Church the book had even greater prominence. The Emperor Charlemagne made it obligatory for the bishops in a series of Synods held at his command, and Archbishop Hincmar of Rheims says it was customary to give the *Regula Pastoralis* into the hands of bishops at their consecration.[2] The modern bishop may envy the days when a textbook, at once profound and practical, was put into his hands to help him in a new and strange way of life.

For myself I read the *Regula Pastoralis* in the weeks before my own consecration as a bishop, and while its practical counsels are remote from our own times it recalls a great ideal. Despite the great differences between his days and our own, the life of Gregory the Great exemplifies still the range and role of the bishop's office. He cared intensely about the spiritual movements, monastic and other, within the Church of his day; and at the same time he had an eye upon the impact of the Church upon the whole community. He was the teacher of the clergy and the people; and at the same time he was a missionary leader, as Gaul and England will never forget. And while he did not shrink from the tasks of administration, he never forgot the contemplative call which had been his in earlier days.

I suggested in the second chapter of this book that the priest's role is a representative one in relation to the whole

[1] Alcuin, *Letters* 116.
[2] Cf. Davis, op. cit., pp. 10–11.

95

Church, a role in which he *displays, enables* and *involves* the Church's character and mission.[1] In that way the priest has his significance as the man of theology, the man of prayer, the man of absolution, and the man of the Eucharist. But because the Church is apostolic and catholic the priests and the lay people in turn require the bishop to *display*, to *enable*, and to involve the Church in acts representing its catholic and apostolic character.

The bishop is still a priest, and unless he retains the heart and mind of a priest he will be a bad bishop. As man of theology he will teach the clergy and help them in their perplexities. As man of prayer he will help clergy and people to see their vocation in prayer and to practise it. As reconciler he will be perhaps less the absolver of individual penitents than one who unites people and groups and conflicting tendencies in the common service of Christ. As man of liturgy he fulfills his role not only in the Eucharist but in his distinctive office of the laying-on of hands both in ordination and in confirmation. In all these ways he will be the priests' priest and the people's priest. And in all that he does he will remember that his office is *apostolic*. His apostolicity is seen not only in pedigree which he holds but in his role of guiding the Church in its mission towards the world, in its preaching of the gospel, in its service of those who suffer, and in its voice on behalf of righteousness in the world.

While therefore the bishop is always a priest, he is also a "layman", living from and in and for the people of Christ as a whole. Priestly indeed, he will avoid being in the bad sense "clerical". And by his humanity he will represent both the Church's apartness and the Church's identification with the wide concerns of the community.

No joy, however, that falls to the bishop is likely to be

[1] Cf. pp. 6–7.

greater than the joy of "ordaining, sending, and laying on hands". It is here that he will be near indeed to the power and authority of the risen Christ. He will be conscious of the reality of which John Keble wrote:

A mortal youth I saw
Nigh to Christ's altar draw
And lowly kneel, while o'er him pastoral hands
Were spread with many a prayer,
And when he rose up there
He could undo or bind the dread celestial bands.

When bread and wine he takes
And of Christ's Passion makes
Memorial high before the mercy throne,
Faith speaks, and we are sure
That offering good and pure
Is more than angels' bread to all whom Christ will own.

What is that silent might
Making the darkness light,
New wine our waters, heavenly blood our wine?
Christ with his mother dear
And all his saints is here
And where they dwell is heaven, and what they touch divine.

A bishop will help the priests to realize "into how high a dignity, and to how weighty an office and charge they are called: that is to say, to be Messengers, Watchmen and Stewards of the Lord", and to know the humility which alone vindicates an authority which is of heaven and not of men.

Yet the bishop will know that an unchanging supernatural authority commends itself only by its ability to speak to each generation, and the ability to speak goes with the readiness to listen and to learn. So the bishop will be the listener,

97

listening not least to those who are younger than himself and watching the new and uprising movements of thought and action in his own Church, in other Churches, and beyond. If for instance he listens and learns in relation to Churches overseas he will see, as others may not see, how painfully insular and introverted the Church in his own country can be. He will be a minister of unity, interpreting his own Church to others and others to his own, and encouraging those who interpret Christian faith to secular minds and secular minds to Christian faith. He will be aware of the upheavals in contemporary society. But at the same time he will know enough history to avoid facile enthusiasm for novelties fot their own sake, and enough of the deeper things of theology to distinguish what is shallow and superficial from what is likely to be lasting. As the keeper of the tradition of Christ he will know what are the things which are not shaken.

It is not surprising that at a time when the role of the priest and the forms which that role takes are seeing change, variety, and experiment, the same should be true of the forms of episcopacy. I do not here discuss dioceses large or small, and the bishop who is the sole father in God, or the bishop whose office is shared with others in a college. Whatever be the shape or form, the bishop will always be pastor, teacher, missionary, sacramental minister, the servant of catholicity and apostolicity amongst priests and people. He must keep fresh, think, read, study, pray. The wise bishop guards what is called "the one in four rule": he has one Sunday in every four free from preaching and other engagements and keeps the day quietly at home.

And what of joy and sorrow? I recall some words which I was moved to use just before I entered upon my present bishopric. "People ask, sometimes, am I in good heart about being Archbishop of Canterbury? My answer is 'yes'. I'm going to it right gladly, to carry out my duty. But the phrase 'in good heart' sometimes gives me pause, because, after all, we are here as a Church to represent Christ crucified and the compassion of Christ crucified before the world. Because that is so, it may be the will of God that our Church should have its heart broken, and if that were to happen it wouldn't mean that we were heading for the world's misery but quite likely pointing the way to the deepest joy".[1]

[1] *About Religion* ed. Michael Redington, Macdonald, 1963.

15

THE GOD WHO CALLS

"Call" is one of the Bible's great words, and it is so because often the subject of the sentence is God. The God of the old and of the new covenant called the world into existence as Creator, and calls men and women to himself as Redeemer. The New Testament writers ascribe the wonderful privileges enjoyed by the Christians as originating in God's call, and the members of the Church are exhorted to praise God for it and to live worthily of it. Within the people of God whom God has called, there are specific calls to particular actions, works and ministry. Thus Paul, and not only Paul, is called to be an apostle. No doubt the readiness of members of the Church to respond to particular calls would depend upon the depth of their realization of the supreme call whereon their faith is founded.

Such is the theological background to the discussions of "vocation" in our contemporary Church. A phrase like "a decline in the number of vocations" needs to be used with caution and with awareness of the spiritual issues. Is God calling less than in the past? Are we sure of the answer to that? Or is God calling to things of which we are unaware? It is clearly possible that both the call of God to a person and the response to it may be hindered or distorted by various factors around him in the Church or elsewhere. No doubt a Church spiritually sensitive and awake to the call to which it owes its own existence would be a Church where special calls were the more heard.

The call of God is to a person, and this involves the heart, the mind, the conscience and the will. No doubt God calls in rather different ways to different people. To some there may be an overwhelming sense of divine imperative pressing upon the conscience. To others, the call may be one which stirs the mind to deep and enquiring thought. To others, the call may be to the feeling of compassion for one's fellows in the world, a compassion shared with the compassion of God. Often the call may be a call to be with Jesus, and being with him to share in his ministry, not least towards those in need or distress. The Church's thoughtful awareness of the many aspects of call and response may help the understanding of the issue and the practical listening and responding.

"Is this man truly called?" The Church has its procedures for deciding the acceptance or otherwise of a person for ordination to the priesthood. Here, if mistakes are made (and there can be no infallibilism) there may be a confusion of two questions. The one question is whether X has been called by God and wants to respond to the call. The other question is whether X looks like the sort of person we want as a priest in our Church. The questions are different ones, because training lies between them; and training means not just the adding of bits of knowledge (however important) to the knowledge possessed already, but the making of the person different. Simon named Peter was called by the sea of Galilee, but how many spiritual misadventures and recoveries there were between the call and the entrance into the apostolic mission.

The heart of training for the priesthood is theology. Theology is the study and knowledge of the divine revelation in which Jesus is the centre. Theology involves the vigorous use of the mind in a range of important studies, and in these studies the universities have given notable leadership, not least in the relating of theology to other mental disciplines. For depth of study there is no substitute. But that knowledge of God which is the meaning of theology calls also for prayer and worship and practical service, and for the contemplation of the truth which is studied. Through the centuries, Christians have found God in cloud and darkness, in the silence of the desert, in serving humanity, and all linked with the studies of the mind. We can be thankful that at the present time there is renewal of the link between theology and spirituality.

The pattern of Christian theology may be described in a number of ways, and one way is in the prologue to the Gospel of John.

In the beginning was the Word, and the Word was with God, and the Word was God. He was in the beginning with God; all things were made through him, and without him was not anything made that was made. In him was life, and the life was the light of men. The light shines in the darkness, and the darkness has not overcome it.

There was a man sent from God, whose name was John. He came for testimony, to bear witness to the light, that all might believe through him. He was not the light, but came to bear witness to the light.

The true light that enlightens every man was coming into the world. He was in the world, and the world was made through him, yet the world knew him not. He came to his own home, and his own people received him not. But to all who received him, who believed in his name, he gave power to become children of God; who were born, not of blood nor of the will of the flesh nor of the will of man, but of God.

And the Word became flesh and dwelt among us, full of grace and truth; we have beheld his glory, the glory as of the only Son from the Father.

Through the Word, God has created the world and given life to it. To mankind the life means the light of mental and moral understanding. Christian theology includes this study of divine activity in the world widely, for beyond the orbit of Israel and Christianity God has made himself known in many cultures and religions. We study the truth of this and its limitations. Meanwhile darkness has come, the agony of moral blindness and evil. Here theology has much to say. Yet the light is not extinguished, nor the desire of many for the fulfilment of God's purpose in the world—however God may be denied by many. Into this many-sided scene Jesus came, with John the Baptist as witness to him, and Jesus is himself the Word through whom God created the world. Jesus is the Word made flesh, uniting himself with humanity. The coming into history of Jesus the Word reveals the divine glory and, when we read further in the Gospel of John, we find that the glory is the splendour of God seen in the self-giving love of the death and resurrection of Jesus. This revelation brings grace—the divine help to mankind in doing God's will, and truth—the truth about God and mankind.

Such is a glimpse of Christian theology. Clearly its understanding involves the use of vigorous intellectual disciplines. History is needed to explore the events, and ethics are needed to consider "the light that lightens every man". Philosophy will have things to say about the phrase "in the beginning", and others too. Yet together with such intellectual disciplines there will be awe and wonder, prayer and worship. The divine glory seen in the death and resurrection of Jesus tells of human suffering transfigured and human lives changed. Such is the range of Christian theology.

We have thought of the meaning of vocation in relation to the God who calls, and of the meaning of theology in the training of the priest. Let this chapter end with some thoughts about the relation of Jesus and the disciples as depicted in the Gospel story.

St Mark, in chapter 3 of his Gospel, tells of a significant day in the lives of the disciples. "And he went up on the mountain, and called to him those whom he desired; and they came to him. And he appointed twelve, to be with him, and to be sent out to preach and have authority to cast out demons." Then follow the names of the twelve. We note that from a larger company whom he summoned the smaller number were specifically appointed; and we note that their appointment is for two ends: first, to be with Jesus and, second, to be sent out. It seems a rhythm of alternating activity, being with Jesus and being sent, and in chapter 6 Mark tells of one of the occasions. After being sent they return, and report what they have done and what they have taught, and Jesus bids them rest a while. Here is the alternating pattern of being with Jesus and being sent.

After the death, resurrection and ascension of Jesus, and the gift of the Holy Spirit, the pattern is changed. The twelve, and others too, are sent, and their mission in the service of the gospel leads them into many lands. But now there is no returning for periods with Jesus, because Jesus is always with them, the crucified and risen Lord. Their ministry has now a deeper relation to Jesus than ever, deeper because of his continuing presence and deeper because they now share in his dying and rising again.

How does this bear upon our own ministry? We recall Galilean scenes which never cease to have meaning and validity for us, but it is the later pattern which is our own. In our ministry the crucified and risen Jesus is ever with us. We are aware of him in the Eucharist, in times of prayer and quiet contemplation (and would that these times were more frequent). He is with us no less among sinners and sufferers, and in our own troubles and anxieties. He is with us not only to inspire us, but to enable us to be sharing in his own ministry. Our caring for the people is our sharing in the present work of Jesus the Shepherd. Our prayer is a sharing in the continuing intercession of Jesus. Our proclamation of the truth of God is our showing to the people Jesus, who is himself the truth.

So the God who calls and is the author of our vocation is the God whose theology we study and teach, and the God who never ceases to be with us as we make him known.

16

PRIESTHOOD: JESUS AND THE
PEOPLE OF GOD

In the books of the New Testament the title priest is never given to the ministry: apostles or bishops or presbyters are never called priests. If they had been so described in the early days of Christianity, it might have suggested a kind of continuation of the Levitical priests of the old covenant, and that old order had been totally superseded by the new concept of priesthood in the person of Christ himself. Indeed, in the New Testament there are two uses of the word priest in relation to Christianity: Jesus Christ himself is priest, and the whole Church is a priesthood.

It is in the Epistle to the Hebrews that the unique priesthood of Jesus is expounded. The book is less a letter than a treatise, and a profound one. As in the Fourth Gospel the glory of Jesus in his life and death reveals the glory of self-giving love in the eternal life of God, so in the Epistle to the Hebrews the sacrifice on the Cross is wrought "through eternal spirit", and the thought is that it reveals a characteristic of sacrifice within the eternal life of deity. In history, Christ's sacrifice was the death on Calvary, once for all and unrepeatable.

Now Christ lives and intercedes in the ascended life, which is ever the life that once died.

However, while the central theme is the sacrifice on Calvary, the book tells, by a number of allusions, of the life of Jesus as a life utterly one with humanity in suffering and in temptation, while being sinless. Christ was "made like his brethren in every respect" and "because he himself has suffered and been tempted, he is able to help those who are tempted". So, too, Jesus "offered up prayers and supplications, with loud cries and tears, to him who was able to save him from death, and he was heard for his godly fear". In these and other passages Christ the priest is no less Christ the pastor, caring for humanity in loving identification. The final blessing at the end of the book, in the midst of sacrificial imagery about Jesus, describes him as "the great shepherd of the sheep", raised to life by the God of peace.

Unique and unrepeatable is Christ's priesthood; but if we shrink from saying that Christians are to share in it, we seem compelled to say that Christians are called to reflect it. If indeed Christians are "partakers of Christ" as this Epistle says, and if they are "carrying about in the body the dying of Jesus" as St Paul says, then his priesthood and sacrifice, unique as they are, are to be reflected in the Christians, and so it is not surprising that another book amongst the New Testament writings tells of priesthood and sacrifice as describing the life of the Church itself.

It is the First Epistle of Peter which draws out the theme of the priesthood of the whole Church. Written to a number of Churches in Asia Minor, by one who addressed them in terms of apostolic authority, this letter is thought by many scholars to have St Peter as its author. The writer dwells upon the death and resurrection of Jesus as the foundation of the Christian faith and as the ground of the Christian hope, and he draws out many practical implications for Christian living and dying, not least in a time of persecution. And in the course of these teachings he describes the Christian Church as a priesthood:

> Come to him, to that living stone, rejected by men but in God's sight chosen and precious; and like living stones be yourselves built into a spiritual house, to be a holy priesthood, to offer spiritual sacrifices acceptable to God through Jesus Christ. (1 Peter 2.4–5)

It is hard to doubt that the spiritual sacrifices offered by the Christians include their worship, their daily Christian life, and their facing of persecution. The writer continues:

> You are a chosen race, a royal priesthood, a holy nation, God's own people, that you may declare the wonderful deeds of him who called you out of darkness into his marvellous light. (1 Peter 2.9)

Between Jesus crucified and risen, and the Church which is the royal priesthood, there are all the means of grace which Christianity possesses: the living Word, the Holy Spirit, the sacraments and the work of the ministry, of which indeed this letter is a striking example. And among these means of grace, the ministry both of apostles and presbyters has its place. The whole letter illustrates a ministry of apostolic authority, and in the final chapter this is related to the ministry of presbyters also.

> So I exhort the elders among you, as a fellow elder and a witness of the sufferings of Christ as well as a partaker in the glory that is to be revealed. Tend the flock of God that is your charge, not by constraint but willingly, not for shameful gain but eagerly, not as domineering over those in your charge but being examples to the flock. And when

108

the chief Shepherd is manifested you will obtain the unfading crown of glory. (1 Peter 5.1–4)

Possessing apostolic authority, the writer shares his ministry with that of the presbyters. They are no doubt appointed by the local Churches and represent them in their worship of God. But linked with the apostles they act in God's name from beyond the Church and, in the name of Jesus crucified and risen, they enable the Church to be indeed the Church of God and to fulfill its mission as the royal priesthood.

So Hebrews and 1 Peter tell of the priesthood of Christ and the priesthood of the Church. The ordained ministry serves both, and indeed will have authority from both. Not surprisingly St Paul, who would never describe himself as a priest, could use priestly language in telling of his own Christian life, and indeed in one passage he describes his preaching to the Gentiles as a sacrificial offering:

> The grace given me by God to be a minister of Christ Jesus to the Gentiles in the priestly service of the gospel of God, so that the offering of the Gentiles may be acceptable, sanctified by the Holy Spirit. (Rom. 15.15–16)

In other passages, too, St Paul uses the language of sacrifice to tell of the Christian life. He bids the Christians in Rome to "present your bodies as a living sacrifice, holy and acceptable to God, which is your spiritual worship" (Rom. 12.1), and he tells the Philippians that he would not grieve if he were offered upon the sacrifice of their faith (Phil. 2.17).

The story of the development of the Christian ministry is familiar enough. There came in the second century the distinction of bishop and presbyter, and the recognition of the apostolic character of the bishop as guardian of the faith

(Irenaeus) and as representing the Church Catholic within the local Church, especially in the celebration of the Eucharist (Ignatius). Thus there emerges the three-fold ministry of bishop, presbyter and deacon. It is the role of bishop and presbyter to represent the local Church, and also the Church universal in and to the local Church, and the authority of Christ crucified and risen in relation to all. In the third century there comes the general attaching of the title "priest" first to bishops and subsequently to presbyters, and the evidence for this development is seen in the Ordinal of Hippolytus and the writings of Cyprian and Tertullian. Though a Levitical analogy appears, as in the use sometimes of the term "high priest", the true balance of relationship between the priesthood of Christ and the priesthood of the whole Church is conserved. Thus in the Eucharist the bishop or presbyter speaks in the name of the local congregation, and in the name of the Church Catholic, and in the name of Jesus himself in his own sacramental action. This depth and balance of theology is seen most vividly in St Augustine in the West and in St Chrysostom in the East. Words of St Augustine are worth quoting:

> The whole redeemed city itself, that is the congregation and society of the Saints, is offered in a universal sacrifice to God through the high priest, who offered himself in suffering for us in the form of a servant, that we might be the body of so great a head. This is the sacrifice of Christians, the one body in Christ, which also the Church celebrates in the sacrament of the altar familiar to the faithful, where it is shown to her that in the thing which she offers she herself is offered.

> (De Civitate Dei 10.6)

After the era of Chrysostom and Augustine there came centuries of development, change and confusion in the concept of priesthood. There was the clericalist trend, which separated the priesthood of the ordained from the priesthood of the Church, which tended to be disregarded; and there was a concentration, somewhat in isolation, upon the priest's Eucharistic function. We need not here trace the confusions and distortions, among which one episode was the condemnation of Anglican Orders by the Church of Rome, first in the sixteenth century and again in 1896. Today the ecumenical movement involves not only the drawing of Churches nearer together, but also the recovery within them of primitive concepts and practice. Here there has been deep recovery of the early conception of the Church's priesthood and the ordained priesthood in relation to it. Both the ARCIC Report and the Lima Report are signs of this recovery. It is a recovery heartening not only for the prospects of Christian unity, but for the deeper understanding of the Church's worship and mission.

So today the ordained priest is called to reflect the priesthood of Christ and to serve the priesthood of the people of God, and to be one of the means of grace whereby God enables the Church to be the Church.

In the Eucharist the Church is very near to the sacrifice of Christ, for the once-for-all offering is brought into the here-and-now by the memorial. While all the people participate, the priest acts in the name of Jesus in the words and actions of the Last Supper, and he represents also the Church as Catholic. So, too, the other parts of his ministry are in Christ's name: his preaching, his absolving, his caring for people in every kind of way, and his witness to the community. Scenes of the mission of Jesus in Galilee and in Judaea are reflected in the ups and downs of his ministry.

At the same time, the ordained priest evokes and serves the ministry of the people of God, and he sees so many of the laity eager to serve and to lead. While he is called to bring the

111

expertise and the authority of his ordination into this scene, he knows that the expertise and the authority are rooted in the humility of Christ.

Cowley Publications is a ministry of the Society of St. John the Evangelist, a religious community for men in the Episcopal Church. Emerging from the Society's tradition of prayer, theological reflection, and diversity of mission, the press is centered in the rich heritage of the Anglican Communion.

Cowley Publications seeks to provide books, audio cassettes, and other resources for the ongoing theological exploration and spiritual development of the Episcopal Church and others in the body of Christ. To this end, it is dedicated to developing a new generation of theological writers, encouraging them to produce timely, creative, and stimulating publications of excellence, and making these publications available widely, reaching both clergy and lay persons.